Homework Workbook

Grade 5

Scott Foresman · Addison Wesley

enVisionMATH™

Scott Foresman is an imprint of

PEARSON

pearsonschool.com

Editorial Offices: Glenview, Illinois • Parsippany, New Jersey • New York, New York
Sales Offices: Boston, Massachusetts • Duluth, Georgia • Glenview, Illinois
Coppell, Texas • Sacramento, California • Chandler, Arizona

ISBN – 13: 978-0-328-34178-8

ISBN – 10: 0-328-34178-9

19 V0N4 15

Table of Contents

Name ______________________________

Place Value

Write the word form for each number and tell the value of the underlined digit.

1. 34,235,345

____

____

2. 19,673,890,004

____

____

3. Write 2,430,090 in expanded form.

____

Write each number in standard form.

4. 80,000,000 + 4,000,000 + 100 + 8 ______________

5. twenty-nine billion, thirty-two million ______________

6. **Number Sense** What number is 10,000 less than 337,676? ______________

7. Which number is 164,502,423 decreased by 100,000?

   A. 164,402,423 **B.** 164,501,423 **C.** 164,512,423 **D.** 264,502,423

8. **Explain It** Explain how you would write 423,090,709,000 in word form.

____

____

____

____

Name ____________________

Practice
1-2

Comparing and Ordering Whole Numbers

Complete. Compare the numbers. Use $<$ or $>$ for each ◯.

1. 23,412 ◯ 23,098

2. 9,000,000 ◯ 9,421,090

Order these numbers from least to greatest.

3. 7,545,999   7,445,999   7,554,000

____

4. **Number Sense** What digit could be in the ten millions place of a number that is less than 55,000,000 but greater than 25,000,000? ____________

5. Put the trenches in order from the least depth to the greatest depth.

____

____

____

____

Depths of Major Ocean Trenches

Trench	Depth (in feet)
Philippine Trench	32,995
Mariana Trench	35,840
Kermadec Trench	32,963
Tonga Trench	35,433

6. These numbers are ordered from greatest to least. Which number could be placed in the second position?

2,643,022   1,764,322   927,322

A 2,743,022   **B** 1,927,304   **C** 1,443,322   **D** 964,322

7. **Explain It** Explain why 42,678 is greater than 42,067.

____

____

____

____

Name ______________________________

Practice 1-3

Decimal Place Value

Write the word form of each number and tell the value of the underlined digit.

1. $3.\underline{1}00$

____

2. $5.2\underline{6}7$

____

3. $2.77\underline{8}$

____

Write each number in standard form.

4. 8 + 0.0 + 0.05 + 0.009 + 0.0006

____

5. 1 + 0.9 + 0.08 + 0.001 + 0.00002

____

Write two decimals that are equivalent to the given decimal.

6. 5.300 ______________

7. 3.7 ______________

8. 0.9 ______________

9. The longest stem on Eli's geranium plant is 7.24 inches. Write 7.24 in word form.

____

____

10. **Explain It** The number 4.124 has two 4s. Why does each 4 have a different value?

____

____

____

Name ______________________

Practice 1-4

Comparing and Ordering Decimals

Write >, <, or = for each ◯.

1. 5.424 ◯ 5.343
2. 0.33 ◯ 0.330
3. 9.489 ◯ 9.479
4. 21.012 ◯ 21.01
5. 223.21 ◯ 223.199
6. 5.43 ◯ 5.432

Order these numbers from least to greatest.

7. 8.37, 8.3, 8.219, 8.129 ______________________
8. 0.012, 0.100, 0.001, 0.101 ______________________
9. **Number Sense** Name three numbers between 0.33 and 0.34.

____

10. Which runner came in first place?

____

11. Who ran faster, Amanda or Steve?

____

12. Who ran for the longest time?

____

Half-Mile Run

Runner	Time (minutes)
Amanda	8.016
Calvin	7.049
Liz	7.03
Steve	8.16

13. Which number is less than 28.43?

A 28.435 **B** 28.34 **C** 28.430 **D** 29.43

14. **Explain It** Explain why it is not reasonable to say that 4.23 is less than 4.13.

____

____

____

Name ______________________________

Problem Solving: Look for a Pattern

Determine the pattern and then complete the grids.

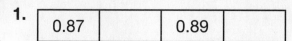

1.

0.87		0.89	

2.

0.22	0.23		

3.

0.12
0.22

4.

0.56
0.76

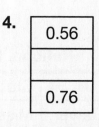

5. **Critical Thinking** In a list of numbers, the pattern increases by 0.001 as you move to the right. If the third number in the list is 0.064, what is the first number in the list? Explain how you know.

____

____

6. If 5 school buses arrive, each carrying exactly 42 passengers, which expression would you use to show how many people in all arrived on the school buses?

A 42 + 5 **B** 42 − 5 **C** 42 × 5 **D** 42 ÷ 5

7. **Explain It** Mishell arranged her coins in the following pattern: $0.27, $0.29, $0.31, $0.33. Explain what her pattern is, and then tell what the next amount of coins would be.

____

____

me ______________________

Mental Math

Show how you can use mental math to add or subtract.

1. 70 + 90 + 30 = ____________ **2.** 350 − 110 = ____________

National Monuments

Name	State	Acres
George Washington Carver	Missouri	210
Navajo	Arizona	360
Fort Sumter	South Carolina	200
Russell Cave	Alabama	310

3. How many more acres are there at Navajo monument than at George Washington Carver monument? ____________

4. How many acres are there at Fort Sumter and Russell Cave combined? ____________

5. Fresh Market bought 56 lb of apples in August from a local orchard. In September, the market purchased an additional 52 lb of apples and 32 lb of strawberries. How many pounds of fruit did the market buy?

A 108 lb **B** 140 lb **C** 150 lb **D** 240 lb

6. Explain It Write the definition and give an example of the Commutative Property of Addition.

____

____

____

Name ______________________

Practice
2-2

Rounding Whole Numbers and Decimals

Round each number to the place of the underlined digit.

1. 32.$\underline{6}$0 ______________

2. 48$\underline{9}$,334,209 ______________

3. 32$\underline{4}$,650 ______________

4. 32.$\underline{0}$73 ______________

5. Reasoning Name two different numbers that round to 30 when rounded to the nearest ten.

____

In 2000, Italy produced 7,464,000 tons of wheat, and Pakistan produced 21,079,000 tons of wheat. Round each country's wheat production in tons to the nearest hundred thousand.

6. Italy ______________

7. Pakistan ______________

The price of wheat in 1997 was $3.38 per bushel. In 1998, the price was $2.65 per bushel. Round the price per bushel of wheat for each year to the nearest tenth of a dollar.

8. 1997 ______________

9. 1998 ______________

10. Number Sense Which number rounds to 15,700,000 when rounded to the nearest hundred thousand?

A 15,000,000 **B** 15,579,999 **C** 15,649,999 **D** 15,659,999

11. Explain It Write a definition of rounding in your own words.

____

____

Name ______________________

Practice
2-3

Estimating Sums and Differences

Estimate each sum or difference.

1. 5,602 − 2,344 ______ **2.** 7.4 + 3.1 + 9.8 ______

3. 2,314 + 671 ______ **4.** 54.23 − 2.39 ______

5. Number Sense Wesley estimated 5.82 − 4.21 to be about 2. Is this an overestimate or an underestimate? Explain.

______

______

6. Estimate the total precipitation in inches and the total number of days with precipitation for Asheville and Wichita.

______

Average Yearly Precipitation of U.S. Cities

City	Inches	Days
Asheville, North Carolina	47.71	124
Wichita, Kansas	28.61	85

7. Reasonableness Which numbers should you add to estimate the answer to this problem: 87,087 + 98,000?

A 88,000 + 98,000 **C** 87,000 + 98,000

B 85,000 + 95,000 **D** 80,000 + 90,000

8. Explain It Estimate the total weight of two boxes that weigh 9.4 lb and 62.6 lb using rounding and compatible numbers. Which estimate is closer to the actual total weight? Why?

______

______

______

Name ______________________

Problem Solving: Draw a Picture and Write an Equation

Write two different equations; then solve each problem.

1. Dayana picked apples for 2 hours. She picked 28 apples in the first hour, and at the end of two hours, she had 49. How many apples did she pick during the second hour? ______________

2. Dixon bought a pack of pencils and then gave 12 away. He now has 24 left. How many pencils were in the pack of pencils that Dixon bought? ______________

Copy and complete the picture. Then write an equation and solve.

3. Rumina is baking 25 muffins for the bake sale. She has already baked 12. How many more does she need to bake?

____

4. **Estimation** Janet saved 22 dollars one month and 39 dollars the next month. She wants to buy a bicycle that costs $100. About how much more money does she need?

   A about $40 **B** about $50 **C** about $60 **D** about $70

5. **Explain It** Stefany ran 2 miles each day for 14 days. How many miles did she run in 14 days? Explain two different ways to solve this problem, and then solve.

____

____

Name ______________________________

Practice

2-5

Adding and Subtracting

Add or subtract.

1. 29,543 + 13,976

2. 93,210 − 21,061

3. 369,021 − 325,310

4. 893,887 + 22,013

5. 971,234 + 55,423 = ______________

6. **Number Sense** Is 4,000 a reasonable estimate for the difference of 9,215 − 5,022? Explain.

____

For questions **7** and **8**, use the table at right.

7. How many people were employed as public officials and natural scientists?

____

8. How many more people were employed as university teachers than as lawyers and judges?

____

People Employed in U.S. by Occupation in 2000

Occupation	Workers
Public officials	753,000
Natural scientists	566,000
University teachers	961,000
Lawyers and judges	926,000

9. Which is the difference between 403,951 and 135,211?

A 200,000 **B** 221,365 **C** 268,740 **D** 539,162

10. **Explain It** Issac is adding 59,029 and 55,678. Should his answer be greater than or less than 100,000? Explain how you know.

____

____

Name ___________________________

Practice
2-6

Adding Decimals

Add.

1. $\begin{array}{r} 58.0 \\ +\ 3.6 \\ \hline \end{array}$

2. $\begin{array}{r} 40.5 \\ +\ 22.3 \\ \hline \end{array}$

3. $\begin{array}{r} 34.587 \\ +\ 21.098 \\ \hline \end{array}$

4. $\begin{array}{r} 43.1000 \\ +\ 8.4388 \\ \hline \end{array}$

5. 16.036 + 7.009 = ____________

6. 92.30 + 0.32 = ____________

7. **Number Sense** Reilly adds 45.3 and 3.21. Should his sum be greater than or less than 48? Tell how you know.

____

____

____

In science class, students weighed different amounts of tin. Carmen weighed 4.361 g, Kim weighed 2.704 g, Simon weighed 5.295 g, and Angelica weighed 8.537 g.

8. How many grams of tin did Carmen and Angelica have combined?

____

9. How many grams of tin did Kim and Simon have combined?

____

10. In December the snowfall was 0.03 in. and in January it was 2.1 in. Which was the total snowfall?

A 3.2 in. **B** 2.40 in. **C** 2.13 in. **D** 0.03 in.

11. **Explain It** Explain why it is important to line up decimal numbers by their place value when you add or subtract them.

____

____

____

Name ______________________

Practice **2-7**

Subtracting Decimals

Subtract.

1. $\begin{array}{r} 92.1 \\ -\ 32.6 \\ \hline \end{array}$ **2.** $\begin{array}{r} 52.7 \\ -\ 36.9 \\ \hline \end{array}$ **3.** $\begin{array}{r} 85.76 \\ -\ 12.986 \\ \hline \end{array}$ **4.** $\begin{array}{r} 32.7 \\ -\ 2.328 \\ \hline \end{array}$

5. 8.7 − 0.3 = ____________ **6.** 23.3 − 1.32 = ____________

7. Number Sense Kelly subtracted 2.3 from 20 and got 17.7. Explain why this answer is reasonable.

____

____

At a local swim meet, the second-place swimmer of the 100-m freestyle had a time of 9.33 sec. The first-place swimmer's time was 1.32 sec faster than the second-place swimmer. The third-place time was 13.65 sec.

8. What was the time for the first-place swimmer? ____________

9. What was the difference in time between the second- and third-place swimmers? ____________

10. Miami's annual precipitation in 2000 was 61.05 in. Albany's was 46.92 in. How much greater was Miami's precipitation than Albany's?

A 107.97 in. **B** 54.31 in. **C** 14.93 in. **D** 14.13 in.

11. Explain It Explain how to subtract 7.6 from 20.39.

____

____

____

____

____

Name ____________________

Practice
2-8

Problem Solving: Multiple-Step Problems

Solve.

1. Theater tickets for children cost $5. Adult tickets cost $3 more. If 2 adults and 2 children buy theater tickets, what is the total cost?

____

2. Luis has a $10 bill and three $5 bills. He spends $12.75 on the entrance fee to an amusement park and $8.50 on snacks. How much money does he have left?

____

3. **Number Sense** Alexandra earns $125 from her paper route each month, but she spends about $20 each month on personal expenses. To pay for a school trip that costs $800, about how many months does she need to save money? Explain.

____

____

4. **Critical Thinking** Patty is a member of the environmental club. Each weekday, she volunteers for 2 hours. On Saturday and Sunday, she volunteers 3 hours more each day. Which expression shows how to find the number of hours she volunteers in one week?

   A 2 + 5

   B 2 + 2 + 2 + 2 + 2 + 5 + 5

   C 2 + 2 + 2 + 3 + 3

   D 2 + 3 + 3

5. **Explain It** An adult's goal is to eat only 2,000 calories each day. One day for breakfast he consumed 310 calories, for lunch he consumed 200 more calories than breakfast, and for dinner he consumed 800. Did he make his goal? Explain.

____

Name ____________________

Multiplication Properties

In **1** through **5**, write the multiplication property used in each equation.

1. $53 \times 6 = 6 \times 53$ ____________________

2. $0 \times 374{,}387 = 0$ ____________________

3. $5 \times (11 \times 4) = (5 \times 11) \times 4$ ____________________

4. $42 \times 1 = 42$ ____________________

5. $14 \times 5 = 5 \times 14$ ____________________

6. **Reasoning** Chan bought 2 large frozen yogurts at $1.50 each and 1 small bottle of water for $1.00. How much did she pay in total?

____

7. Dan has 4 shelves. He has exactly 10 books on each shelf. Judy has 10 shelves. She has exactly 4 books on each shelf. Who has more books? Explain.

____

____

8. **Algebra** If $3 \times 8 \times 12 = 8 \times 3 \times n$, what is the value of n?

A 3 **B** 8 **C** 12 **D** 18

9. **Explain It** Write a definition for the Associative Property of Multiplication in your own words and explain how you would use it to compute $4 \times 25 \times 27$ mentally.

____

____

____

____

Name ______________________

Practice 3-2

Using Mental Math to Multiply

Use mental math to find each product.

1. $150 \times 20 =$ ______

2. $0 \times 50 \times 800 =$ ______

3. $500 \times 40 =$ ______

4. $120 \times 50 =$ ______

5. $60 \times 70 \times 1 =$ ______

6. $9{,}000 \times 80 =$ ______

7. $100 \times 10 \times 1 =$ ______

8. $1{,}800 \times 20 \times 0 =$ ______

9. $30 \times 20 =$ ______

10. $1{,}400 \times 2{,}000 =$ ______

11. $7{,}000 \times 50 \times 1 =$ ______

12. $1{,}000 \times 200 \times 30 =$ ______

13. Number Sense A googol is a large number that is the digit one followed by one hundred zeros. If you multiply a googol by 100, how many zeros will that product have?

______

14. Gregorios drives 200 miles per day for 10 days. How many miles did he drive in all?

______

15. Algebra If $a \times b \times c = 0$, and a and b are integers greater than 10, what must c equal?

A 0 **B** 1 **C** 2 **D** 10

16. Explain It SungHee empties her piggy bank and finds that she has 200 quarters, 150 dimes, and 300 pennies. How much money does she have? Explain.

______

______

Name ______________________

Practice
3-3

Estimating Products

Estimate each product.

1. 68 × 21 = ______

2. 5 × 101 = ______

3. 151 × 21 = ______

4. 99 × 99 = ______

5. 87 × 403 = ______

6. 19 × 718 = ______

7. 39 × 51 = ______

8. 47 × 29 × 11 = ______

9. 70 × 27 = ______

10. 69 × 21 × 23 = ______

11. 7 × 616 = ______

12. 8,880 × 30 = ______

13. Number Sense Give three numbers whose product is about 9,000.

____

Electronics Prices

CD player	$ 74.00
MP3 player	$ 99.00
CD/MP3 player	$199.00
AM/FM radio	$ 29.00

14. About how much would it cost to buy 4 CD/MP3 players and 3 MP3 players?

____

15. Which is the closest estimate for the product of 2 × 19 × 5?

A 1,150 **B** 200 **C** 125 **D** 50

16. Explain It Explain how you know whether an estimate of a product is an overestimate or an underestimate.

____

____

____

____

Name ______________________________

Practice 3-4

Multiplying by 1-Digit Numbers

Find each product. Estimate to check that your answer is reasonable.

1. $58 \times 3 =$ ______________

2. $49 \times 8 =$ ______________

3. $83 \times 5 =$ ______________

4. $95 \times 6 =$ ______________

5. $273 \times 4 =$ ______________

6. $35 \times 8 =$ ______________

7. $789 \times 6 =$ ______________

8. $643 \times 7 =$ ______________

9. $\begin{array}{r} 68 \\ \times\ 2 \\ \hline \end{array}$

10. $\begin{array}{r} 582 \\ \times\ 5 \\ \hline \end{array}$

11. $\begin{array}{r} 84 \\ \times\ 4 \\ \hline \end{array}$

12. $\begin{array}{r} 926 \\ \times\ 7 \\ \hline \end{array}$

13. Xavier painted five portraits and wants to sell them for 36 dollars each. How much money will he make if he sells all five? ______________

14. A farmer wants to build a square pigpen. The length of one side of the pen is 13 ft. How many feet of fencing should the farmer buy? ______________

15. Jasmine wants to buy 4 green bags for 18 dollars each and 3 purple bags for 15 dollars each. She has 100 dollars. How much more money does she need? ______________

16. **Geometry** A regular octagon is a figure that has eight sides with equal lengths. If one side of a regular octagon is 14 inches long, what is the perimeter of the entire octagon?

A 148 in. **B** 140 in. **C** 112 in. **D** 84 in.

17. **Explain It** Why is 2,482 not a reasonable answer for 542×6?

____

____

____

Name ______________________

Practice
3-5

Multiplying 2-Digit by 2-Digit Numbers

Find each product. Estimate to check that your answer is reasonable.

1. 56×34

2. 45×76

3. 35×15

4. 47×94

5. 64×51

6. 47×30

7. 56×19

8. 92×49

9. To pay for a sofa, Maddie made a payment of 64 dollars each month for one year. How much did the sofa cost ? ______________

10. Geometry To find the volume of a box, you multiply the length times the width times the height. What is the volume, in cubic feet, of a box that is 3 ft long, 8 ft wide, and 16 ft high? ______________

11. Estimation Katie is in charge of buying juice for the teachers' breakfast party. If one teacher will drink between 18 and 22 ounces of juice, and there are 32 teachers, which is the best estimate for the amount of juice Katie should buy?

A about 200 ounces
B about 400 ounces
C about 600 ounces
D about 800 ounces

12. Explain It Is 7,849 a reasonable answer for 49×49? Why or why not?

____

____

____

Name ______________________

Multiplying Greater Numbers

Find each product. Estimate to check that your answer is reasonable.

1. 556×34

2. 234×75

3. 395×76

4. 483×57

5. 628×33

6. 154×35

7. 643×49

8. 536×94

9. Number Sense In a class of 24 students, 13 students sold over 150 raffle tickets each, and the rest of the class sold about 60 raffle tickets each. The class goal was to sell 2,000 tickets. Did they reach their goal? Explain.

____

____

____

10. Player A's longest home run distance is 484 ft. If Player A hits 45 home runs at his longest distance, what would the total distance be? ______________

11. Player B's longest home run distance is 500 ft. There are 5,280 ft in 1 mi. How many home runs would Player B need to hit at his longest distance for the total to be greater than 1 mi? ______________

12. Algebra Which equation shows how you can find the number of minutes in one year?

A $60 \times 24 \times 365$
B $60 \times 60 \times 24$
C 60×365
D $60 \times 60 \times 365$

13. Explain It Write a real-world problem where you would have to multiply 120 and 75.

____

Name ____________________

Practice 3-7

Exponents

For questions **1–4**, write in exponential notation.

1. $13 \times 13 \times 13$ ____________

2. $8 \times 8 \times 8 \times 8 \times 8 \times 8$ ____________

3. 64×64 ____________

4. $4 \times 4 \times 4 \times 4 \times 4 \times 4 \times 4 \times 4$ ____________

For questions **5–8**, write in expanded form.

5. 2^5 ____________

6. 20 squared ____________

7. 11^4 ____________

8. 9 cubed ____________

For questions **9–12**, write in standard form.

9. $4 \times 4 \times 4$ ____________

10. 14 squared ____________

11. 6^5 ____________

12. $9 \times 9 \times 9 \times 9$ ____________

13. Number Sense Which of these numbers, written in expanded form, is equal to 625?

A $5 \times 5 \times 5 \times 5$
B 5×5
C $5 \times 5 \times 5$
D $5 \times 5 \times 5 \times 5 \times 5$

14. Number Sense Find the number equal to 6 raised to the second power.

A 18
B 36
C 6
D 12

15. Explain It Explain what 4 raised to the fourth power means.

____

____

Name ______________________

Practice
3-8

Problem Solving: Draw a Picture and Write an Equation

Draw a picture and write an equation. Then solve.

1. When Mary was born, she weighed 8 pounds. When she was 10 years old, she weighed 10 times as much. How much did she weigh when she was 10 years old?

____

2. Sandi is 13 years old. Karla is 3 times Sandi's age. How old is Karla?

____

3. **Reasoning** Hwong can fit 12 packets of coffee in a small box and 50 packets of coffee in a large box. Hwong has 10 small boxes and would like to reorganize them into large boxes. Which boxes should he use? Explain.

____

____

4. **Number Sense** Daniel has 12 tennis balls. Manuel has twice as many tennis balls as Daniel. Kendra has twice as many balls as Manuel. How many tennis balls do they have in all?

A 24 **B** 36 **C** 84 **D** 96

5. **Explain It** William travels only on Saturdays and Sundays and has flown 400 miles this month. Jason travels every weekday and has flown 500 miles this month. Who travels more miles *per day*? Explain.

____

____

____

Name ______________________

Practice
4-1

Dividing Multiples of 10 and 100

Use mental math to find each quotient.

1. 27 ÷ 9 = ______

2. 270 ÷ 9 = ______

3. 2,700 ÷ 9 = ______

4. 24 ÷ 4 = ______

5. 240 ÷ 4 = ______

6. 2,400 ÷ 4 = ______

7. 720 ÷ 9 = ______

8. 140 ÷ 7 = ______

9. 2,100 ÷ 3 = ______

10. If a bike race covers 120 mi over 6 days and the cyclists ride the same distance each day, how many miles does each cyclist ride each day? ______

Use mental math to answer the following questions.

Dealership Vehicle Storage	
Sections of vehicles	4
Vehicles for sale	1,200
Rows per section	10

11. If the vehicles are divided evenly between the sections, how many vehicles are in each section?

______

12. If the vehicles are divided evenly between the rows in each section, how many vehicles are in each row? ______

13. **Algebra** If 160,000 ÷ n = 4, find n. ______

14. Find 32,000 ÷ 8 mentally.

A 4,000 **B** 400 **C** 40 **D** 4

15. **Explain It** Solve the equation $n \times 50 = 5{,}000$. Explain your solution.

______

Name ______________________

Estimating Quotients

Estimate each quotient. Tell which method you used.

1. 195 ÷ 4 __________ __________

2. 283 ÷ 5 __________ __________

3. 766 ÷ 8 __________ __________

4. 179 ÷ 2 __________ __________

5. $395.20 ÷ 5 __________ __________

6. $31.75 ÷ 8 __________ __________

7. $247.80 ÷ 5 __________ __________

8. **Reasoning** If you use $63.00 ÷ 9 to estimate $62.59 ÷ 9, is $7.00 greater than or less than the exact answer? Explain.

9. A band played 3 concerts and earned a total of $321.00. The band earned about the same amount for each concert. Estimate how much the band earned each night.

10. At a department store, a woman's total was $284.00 for 7 items. Estimate the average cost per item.

11. Which is the closest estimate for 213 ÷ 4?

A 50 **B** 40 **C** 30 **D** 20

12. **Explain It** Explain how to estimate 524 ÷ 9.

Name ______________________

Problem Solving: Reasonableness

Solve.

1. One tray holds eight sandwiches. If there are 30 sandwiches in all, how many trays are needed?

____

2. There are 53 students on a field trip. One chaperone is needed for every 6 students. How many chaperones are needed?

____

Mrs. Favicchio has 72 students in her science class. The table shows how many students can use each item of lab supplies she is ordering.

Lab Supplies

Item	Number of Students
Packet of pH paper	10
Case of test tubes	5
Case of petri dishes	4

3. How many packets of pH paper does she need to order?

____

4. How many cases of test tubes does she need to order?

____

5. **Algebra** A loaf of banana bread serves 6 guests. There will be 47 guests attending the faculty breakfast. Which expression shows how many loaves are needed to serve them all?

A 47 divided by 6 is 7 R 5, so 7 loaves are needed.

B 47 divided by 6 is 7 R 5, so 8 loaves are needed.

C 47 plus 6 is 53, so 53 loaves are needed.

D 47 minus 6 is 41, so 41 loaves are needed.

6. **Explain It** You are in line at an amusement park. You count 34 people in front of you. Each rollercoaster fits 11 people. How many rollercoasters must run before you can get on? Explain.

____

____

Name ______________________________

Practice
4-4

Connecting Models and Symbols

After mowing lawns for one week, John put the money he earned on the table. There were four $100 bills, three $10 bills, and five $1 bills.

1. If John's brother borrowed one of the $100 bills and replaced it with ten $10 bills,

a. how many $100 bills would there be? ____________

b. how many $10 bills would there be? ____________

2. If John needed to divide the money evenly with two other workers, how much would each person receive? ____________

3. If John needed to divide the money evenly with four other workers, how much would each person receive? ____________

Complete each division problem. You may use play money or draw diagrams to help.

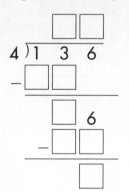

4.

```
      □□
  4)1 3 6
  −□□
    ------
    □ 6
   −□□
    ------
      □
```

5.

```
      □□
  3)1 6 2
  −□□
    ------
    □ 2
   −□□
    ------
      □
```

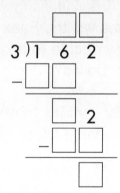

6. If $644.00 is divided equally among 7 people, how much will each person receive?

A $82.00 **B** $92.00 **C** $93.00 **D** $103.00

7. **Explain It** Write a story problem using two $100 bills, nine $10 bills, and seven $1 bills.

____

____

____

____

Name ____________________

Practice **4-5**

Dividing by 1-Digit Divisors

Find each quotient.

1. $2\overline{)586}$ **2.** $3\overline{)565}$ **3.** $5\overline{)718}$ **4.** $4\overline{)599}$

5. $5\overline{)642}$ **6.** $6\overline{)354}$ **7.** $9\overline{)210}$ **8.** $8\overline{)927}$

The Paez family lives in Louisville, Kentucky, and has decided to take a road trip for their summer vacation.

9. How many miles will the Paez family drive each day if they decide to take 5 days to drive 865 mi to Dallas? ____________

10. The Paez family decides they want to drive 996 mi to Boston in 6 days. How many miles will they drive each day? ____________

11. Reasonableness If a staff of 9 people had to clean a hotel with 198 rooms, how many rooms would each person have to clean if they divided the rooms equally?

A 29 **B** 25 **C** 23 **D** 22

12. Explain It Explain how to check the quotient from a division problem.

____

____

____

Name ______________________

Practice
4-6

Zeros in the Quotient

Find each quotient. Check your answers by multiplying.

1. 490 ÷ 7 = ______ **2.** 326 ÷ 3 = ______

3. 916 ÷ 3 = ______ **4.** 720 ÷ 2 = ______

5. $2\overline{)941}$ **6.** $9\overline{)982}$ **7.** $7\overline{)740}$ **8.** $5\overline{)703}$

9. If there are 505 seats in an auditorium divided equally into 5 sections, how many seats are in each section? ______

10. A book company publishes 749 copies of a novel and distributes them to 7 bookstores. If each bookstore were to receive the same number of copies, how many copies would be sent to each store? ______

11. In one year, Dolores and Tom's four children saved $420 by recycling cans. When they divided the money equally, how much money did each child receive?

A $50 **B** $100 **C** $105 **D** $1,500

12. **Explain It** Explain why estimating before you divide 624 ÷ 6 helps you place the first digit in the quotient.

______

______

______

Name ______________________________

Practice 4-7

Understanding Factors

List all the factors of each number.

1. 36 ______________________________

2. 90 ______________________________

3. 84 ______________________________

Number Sense A number is divisible by 4 if the last two digits are divisible by 4. Write yes on the line if the number is divisible by 4 and no if it is not.

4. 324 __________ **5.** 634 __________ **6.** 172 __________

7. A class of 80 students is graduating from elementary school. The teachers need help figuring out how to line up the students for the ceremony. One row of 80 students would be too long. What other ways could the students be arranged for the ceremony?

____

____

8. A number is divisible by another number when the ______________ after division by that number is 0.

9. **Number Sense** What factor pair is missing for 45 if you already know 1 and 45, 5 and 9?

A 7 and 6 **B** 8 and 6 **C** 3 and 15 **D.** 4 and 12

10. **Explain It** Explain how to find all the factor pairs of 40.

____

____

____

____

Name ______________________

Practice 4-8

Prime and Composite Numbers

Write whether each number is prime or composite.

1. 21 ________ **2.** 36 ________ **3.** 31 ________

4. 87 ________ **5.** 62 ________ **6.** 23 ________

Use factor trees to find the prime factorization of each number.

7. 44 ________ **8.** 63 ________

9. 13 ________ **10.** 54 ________

11. Number Sense Audrey says that the prime factorization of 42 is 21 × 2. Is she correct? If not, tell why.

____

____

12. Is 4,564,282 prime or composite? Explain how you determined your answer.

____

____

13. Which of the following is a prime number?

A 105 **B** 27 **C** 19 **D** 9

14. Explain It Does it matter what two factors you select to complete a factor tree? Explain.

____

____

Name ____________________

Problem Solving: Draw a Picture and Write an Equation

Draw a picture and write an equation. Then solve.

1. Tommy paid $39 to fill up the gas tank in his car. If one gallon of gas costs $3, how many gallons of gas did Tommy put in?

____

____

2. To prepare for the brunch, Ivana needs to place 8 muffins in each basket. If she has 115 muffins, how many baskets will she need?

____

____

3. **Write a Problem** Write a real-world problem that you can solve by writing an equation. The answer to the problem must be 6.

____

____

4. **Geometry** The perimeter is the distance around an object. The perimeter of a square is 84 centimeters. What is the length of one side of the square?

   A 75 cm **B** 42 cm **C** 21 cm **D** 14 cm

5. **Explain It** A perfect score on a quiz is 100. Mrs. Frisoli gives students 1 point for putting their name on the paper. If there are only 9 questions on the quiz, how much is each question worth? Explain how you found your answer.

____

____

Name ________________________________

Using Patterns to Divide

In **1** through **4**, find each quotient. Use mental math.

1. 360 ÷ 40 = 36 tens ÷ 4 tens = ____________

2. 5,400 ÷ 90 = 540 tens ÷ 9 tens = ____________

3. 240 ÷ 30 = 24 tens ÷ 3 tens = ____________

4. 4,800 ÷ 10 = 480 tens ÷ 1 ten = ____________

Use mental math to answer the following questions.

Dealership Vehicle Storage	
Sections of vehicles	4
Vehicles for sale	1,200
Rows per section	10

5. If the vehicles are divided evenly among the sections, how many vehicles are in each section?

____

6. If the vehicles are divided evenly among the rows in each section, how many vehicles are in each row?

____

7. Estimation Suppose there are 297 students going on a field trip. If each schoolbus can carry 58 students, estimate the number of buses that will be needed to transport all the students.

____

____

8. Algebra If 160,000 ÷ *n* = 4, what is the value of *n*?

A 40 **B** 400 **C** 4,000 **D** 40,000

9. Explain It Solve the equation *n* × 50 = 5,000. Explain your solution.

____

____

Name ______________________

Practice
5-2

Estimating Quotients with 2-Digit Divisors

In **1** through **4**, estimate the quotients using compatible numbers.

1. 566 ÷ 81 = __________ **2.** 453 ÷ 93 = __________

3. 1,423 ÷ 69 = __________ **4.** 8,631 ÷ 10 = __________

5. Reasoning If you use $99.00 ÷ 11 to estimate $98.69 ÷ 11, is $9.00 greater than or less than the exact answer? Explain.

____

____

6. Suppose there are 19 students in a class. A teacher has 122 pencils and passes them out to the class. Estimate the number of pencils each student will receive. __________

7. At a department store, a package of 12 handkerchiefs costs $58.99. Estimate how much each handkerchief costs. __________

8. Number Sense Which is the closest estimate for 2,130 ÷ 33?

A 7 **B** 17 **C** 70 **D** 700

9. Explain It Explain how to estimate 498 ÷ 12.

____

____

Name ______________________________

Practice
5-3

Problem Solving: Multiple-Step Problems

Write and answer the hidden question. Then solve.

1. Gloria talked on her cell phone for 320 minutes the first month, 243 minutes the second month, and 489 minutes the third month. Her payment package does not allow her to pay per minute; she can only buy packages. If she has to pay $25 for every 200 minutes, how much did she pay for the first three months?

____

____

____

____

2. Each can of paint will cover 450 tiles. Augustin is painting 300 tiles in his bathroom, 675 in his kitchen, and 100 in his hallway. How many cans of paint does he need to buy?

____

____

3. **Number Sense** The sum of three different numbers is 18. If every number is a prime number, what are the three numbers?

____

4. **Explain It** You earn $3 an hour as a waitress. After working 3 hours, you earn $12, $5, and $7 in tips. How much money did you earn in total? Explain how you found your answer.

____

____

Name ______________________

Practice 5-4

Dividing by Multiples of 10

In **1** through **6**, divide.

1. $20\overline{)467}$ ________ **2.** $40\overline{)321}$ ________

3. $80\overline{)813}$ ________ **4.** $40\overline{)284}$ ________

5. $90\overline{)648}$ ________ **6.** $10\overline{)587}$ ________

7. To drive from New York City, NY, to Los Angeles, CA, you must drive about 2,779 miles. If you drive 60 miles per hour without stopping, about how many hours do you have to drive? ________

8. **Reasoning** Suppose one bottle of paint can cover 20 tiles. You have 348 tiles. How many bottles of paint do you need to buy to cover all 348 tiles? Explain.

____

____

9. A group of 483 students is taking a field trip. One bus is needed for every 50 students. How many buses are needed?

____

10. **Geometry** A decagon is a ten-sided figure. If a decagon has a perimeter of 114 centimeters, how long is each side of the figure?

A 11.4 cm **B** 14 cm **C** 114 cm **D** 124 cm

11. **Explain It** To figure out how many hours it will take to drive from his home to his cousin's house, a student divides 289 by 60 and estimates that it will take about 4.5 hours. Explain whether you think this is a reasonable estimate.

____

____

____

Name ______________________

Practice 5-5

1-Digit Quotients

In **1** through **6**, find each quotient.

1. $37\overline{)120}$ **2.** $39\overline{)342}$ **3.** $62\overline{)338}$

4. $42\overline{)284}$ **5.** $82\overline{)599}$ **6.** $55\overline{)474}$

7. Solomon has $118. He wants to purchase concert tickets for himself and 5 friends. Each ticket costs $19. Does he have enough money? Explain.

____

____

8. Number Sense Which problem will have the greater quotient, 376.0 ÷ 93 OR 376 ÷ 93.01? Explain how you know.

____

____

____

9. Which is 458 ÷ 73?

A 5 R19 **B** 5 R20 **C** 6 R19 **D** 6 R20

10. Explain It A student solves the problem 354 ÷ 24. The student finds an answer of 13 R40. Explain how you can tell that the answer is incorrect just by looking at the remainder.

____

____

____

Name ______________________

2-Digit Quotients

In **1** through **6**, find each quotient.

1. $14\overline{)413}$ __________ **2.** $29\overline{)634}$ __________

3. $35\overline{)768}$ __________ **4.** $19\overline{)401}$ __________

5. $45\overline{)942}$ __________ **6.** $26\overline{)503}$ __________

7. Reasoning The school student council sponsored a Switch Day where students were able to switch classes every 20 minutes. The students are in school for 7 hours. If a student switched as often as possible, how many times did that student get to visit another classroom? (Hint: There are 60 minutes in 1 hour.)

____

8. 456 students participated in Switch Day. The students raised money for charity so that the principal would approve of the day. If the total amount of money raised was $912, and each student brought in the same amount of money, how much did each student raise?

____

9. Estimation The total dinner bill at a buffet came out to $589 for 31 people. About how much was the buffet cost per person?

A $15.00 **B** $20.00 **C** $22.00 **D** $25.00

10. Explain It If you have a two-digit divisor and a three-digit dividend, does the quotient always have the same number of digits?

____

____

Name ____________________

Practice 5-7

Estimating and Dividing with Greater Numbers

Estimate first. Then use a calculator to find the quotient. Round to the nearest hundredth if necessary.

1. $53\overline{)6{,}324}$ **2.** $52\overline{)6{,}348}$ **3.** $86\overline{)31{,}309}$ **4.** $33\overline{)3{,}455}$

5. 17,496 ÷ 91 = ____________ **6.** 25,214 ÷ 47 = ____________

7. 2,312 ÷ 26 = ____________ **8.** 4,895 ÷ 83 = ____________

The Humphrey family decided to fly from San Francisco to New York City, and from there to Rome, New Delhi, and finally Tokyo.

9. It took the Humphrey family 6 hr to travel from San Francisco to New York. How many kilometers did they travel per hour?

____

Distances by Plane	
San Francisco to New York	4,140 km
New York to Rome	6,907 km
Rome to New Delhi	5,929 km
New Delhi to Tokyo	5,857 km

10. During the flight from New Delhi to Tokyo, flight attendants came through with snacks every 600 km. How many times did they come through?

____

11. Reasoning Use the data from Exercises 9 and 10. When the family arrived in New Delhi from Rome, the youngest son asked the pilot how fast he was flying the plane. The pilot told him about 847 km per hour. How many hours did it take the family to fly from Rome to New Delhi?

A 5 h **B** 6 h **C** 7 h **D** 8 h

12. Explain It Write a word problem that would require you to use 5,621 ÷ 23.

____

Name ______________________

Practice
5-8

Problem Solving: Missing or Extra Information

Decide if each problem has extra or missing information. Solve if possible.

1. It takes 4 hours to drive from Boston to New York. Jordan has a meeting in New York at 2:00 P.M. Can she arrive at her meeting on time?

____

2. Franco hikes 4 miles each day for 5 days. He carries 100 ounces of water with him. It takes him 1 hour to hike 4 miles. How many hours did he hike in 5 days?

____

3. **Write a Problem** Write a real-world problem that gives extra information. Under the problem write what the extra information is.

____

4. **Critical Thinking** Jorge buys T-shirts for $4 each and paints designs on them. He sells the designed T-shirts for $7 each. What information is needed to find how much profit he makes in one week?

   A The price of T-shirts at a store
   B The color of the T-shirts that he buys
   C The types of designs he draws on the T-shirts
   D The number of T-shirts he sells in one week

5. **Explain It** Krista can type 60 words per minute. She wrote an essay by hand in 5 hours, and it is now 4 pages long and has 500 words in it. She wants to type up her essay. About how long will it take to type her essay? Write what the extra or missing information is. Then solve if possible.

____

____

Name ____________________

Practice 6-1

Variables and Expressions

For questions **1** through **4**, use a variable to write an algebraic expression that represents the word phrase.

1. a number of apples divided into 12 baskets ____________

2. 5 more than s ____________

3. three times the cost for one hat ____________

4. nine fewer than the total number of people ____________

For **5** through **7**, translate each algebraic expression into words.

5. $3 + w$ ____________

6. $8x$ ____________

7. $40 - p$ ____________

8. Write two different word phrases for the expression $\frac{t}{30}$.

____

____

9. **Number Sense** Do $5 + x$ and $x + 5$ represent the same expression? Explain.

____

____

10. **Algebra** Dan is 12 in. taller than Jay. Use x for Jay's height. Which expression shows Dan's height?

A $x + 12$ **B** $x - 12$ **C** $12x$ **D** $\frac{x}{12}$

11. **Explain It** Explain what the expression $6x$ means.

____

Name ____________________

Practice **6-2**

Patterns and Expressions

In **1** through **4**, evaluate each expression for $n = 3$ and $n = 8$.

1. $n + 10$

2. $\frac{24}{n}$

3. $n \times 5$

4. $36 - n$

Complete each table.

5.

n	$0.9 + n$
0.5	
0.2	
0.15	
0.1	

6.

n	$96 \div n$
1	
2	
3	
4	

7. Write a Problem Write a situation that can be represented by the algebraic expression $3.50*t*.

8. Algebra If $a = 10$, which of the following is the correct solution for $a \times 0.1$?

A 0.01 **B** 0.1 **C** 1 **D** 10

9. Explain It Write one numerical expression and one algebraic expression. Then explain what the difference between a numerical and algebraic expression is.

Name ______________________

Practice 6-3

More Patterns and Expressions

1. Write an algebraic expression to represent the cost of a concert ticket, *h*, with a service charge of \$6.75.

____

2. Write an algebraic expression to represent the cost of *m* gallons of gasoline if each gallon costs \$1.45.

____

Evaluate each expression for $n = 3$ and $n = 6$.

3. $0.2 \times n$ ________ ________

4. $n - 2.1$ ________ ________

5. $\frac{12}{n}$ ________ ________

6. $35 + n$ ________ ________

Complete each table.

7.

n	$0.7 + n$
0.5	
0.2	
0.15	
0.1	

8.

n	$60 \div n$
1	
2	
3	
4	

9. **Explain It** What is another way to write the expression $44n$? What is another way to write the expression $44 \div n$?

____

10. Which is the correct product of $n \times 7$ if $n = \$0.25$?

A \$3.25 **B** \$2.75 **C** \$2.25 **D** \$1.75

11. **Write a Problem** Write a situation that can be represented by the algebraic expression \$3.25*d*.

____

Name ______________________________

Practice
6-4

Distributive Property

Use the Distributive Property to multiply mentally.

1. $5 \times 607 =$ ____________ **2.** $16 \times 102 =$ ____________

3. $7 \times 420 =$ ____________ **4.** $265 \times 5 =$ ____________

5. $44 \times 60 =$ ____________ **6.** $220 \times 19 =$ ____________

7. $45 \times 280 =$ ____________ **8.** $341 \times 32 =$ ____________

9. Number Sense Fill in the blanks to show how the Distributive Property can be used to find 10×147.

$10 \times (150 - 3) = (10 \times 150) - ($ ____________ $\times 3) =$

$1{,}500 -$ ____________ $=$ ____________

10. In 1990, there were 1,133 tornadoes in the U.S. If there were the same number of tornadoes for 10 years in a row, what would be the 10-year total?

____

11. There were 1,071 tornadoes in the U.S. in 2000. What is the number of tornadoes multiplied by 20?

____

12. If $4 \times 312 = 4 \times 300 + n$, which is the value of n?

A 4 B 12 C 48 D 300

13. Explain It Margaret said that she used the Distributive Property to solve 4×444. Is her answer shown below correct? Explain.

$4 \times 444 = 4 \times (400 + 40 + 4) =$

$(4 \times 400) + (4 \times 40) + (4 \times 4) =$

$1{,}600 + 160 + 16 = 1{,}776$

____

____

Name ______________________

Practice 6-5

Order of Operations

Use the order of operations to evaluate each expression.

1. $4 \times 4 + 3 =$ ________

2. $3 + 6 \times 2 \div 3 =$ ________

3. $24 - (8 \div 2) + 6 =$ ________

4. $(15 - 11) \times (25 \div 5) =$ ________

5. $26 - 4 \times 5 + 2 =$ ________

6. $15 \times (7 - 7) + (5 \times 2) =$ ________

7. $(8 \div 4) \times (7 \times 0) =$ ________

8. $5 \times (6 - 3) + 10 \div (8 - 3) =$ ________

9. Explain It Which is a true statement, $5 \times 4 + 1 = 25$ or $3 + 7 \times 2 = 17$? Explain your answer.

____

____

Insert parentheses to make each statement true.

10. $25 \div 5 - 4 = 25$ ______________________

11. $7 \times 4 - 4 \div 2 = 26$ ______________________

12. $3 + 5 \times 2 - 10 = 6$ ______________________

13. Strategy Practice Insert parentheses in the expression $6 + 10 \times 2$ so that:

a. the expression equals 32. ______________________

b. the expression equals $(12 + 1) \times 2$. ______________________

14. Solve $(25 - 7) \times 2 \div 4 + 2$.

A 18 **B** 11 **C** 6 **D** 5

15. Write two order-of-operation problems. Then trade with a classmate and solve the problems.

____

____

Name ______________________________

Problem Solving: Act It Out and Use Reasoning

1. Christina collects stamps. She has 47 stamps in all. She has 20 stamps from Europe. The number of African stamps is 2 times the number of Asian stamps. How many stamps from each of these three continents does she have?

____

2. **Write a Problem** Write a problem that can be solved by acting it out and using reasoning.

____

____

____

3. A public pool opened for the summer. A total of 246 people came swimming over the first 3 days it was open. On the first day, 79 came to swim. On the second day, 104 people swam. How many people swam on the third day?

____

4. Marissa earned $480 in the summer. If she earned $40 a week, how many weeks did she work?

A 48 **B** 12 **C** 10 **D** 9

5. **Explain It** How could you use cubes to act out a problem?

____

____

____

____

____

Name ____________________

Practice
7-1

Multiplying Decimals by 10, 100, or 1,000

Use mental math to find each product.

1. 53.7 × 10 ____________

2. 74.3 × 100 ____________

3. 66.37 × 1,000 ____________

4. 1.03 × 10 ____________

5. 92.5 × 10 ____________

6. 0.8352 × 100 ____________

7. 0.567 × 100 ____________

8. 572.6 × 1,000 ____________

9. 5.8 × 100 ____________

10. 0.21 × 1,000 ____________

11. 6.2 × 1,000 ____________

12. 1.02 × 10 ____________

13. 0.003 × 1,000 ____________

14. 0.002 × 10 ____________

15. 7.03 × 10 ____________

16. 4.06 × 100 ____________

17. **Algebra** Kendra bought 10 gallons of gasoline at $3.26 per gallon. How much did she pay for the gasoline?

A $326.00 **B** $32.60 **C** $1.26 **D** $0.26

18. **Strategy Practice** Freddy is helping buy ingredients for salads for the school spaghetti dinner. He bought 10 pounds of onions at $0.69 per pound, 100 pounds of tomatoes at $0.99 pound, 1,000 pounds of bread crumbs at $0.09 per pound, and 100 pounds of lettuce at $0.69 per pound. Which of the items he bought cost the most?

A tomatoes **B** lettuce **C** bread crumbs **D** onions

19. **Explain It** Marco and Suzi each multiplied 0.721 × 100. Marco got 7.21 for his product. Suzi got 72.1 for her product. Which student multiplied correctly? How do you know?

____

____

Name ______________________________

Practice **7-2**

Multiplying a Decimal by a Whole Number

Find each product.

1. 5.4×3

2. 3.8×4

3. 0.55×8

4. 8.19×5

Insert a decimal point in each answer to make the equation true.

5. $5 \times 6.3 = 315$ ____________

6. $3.001 \times 9 = 27009$ ____________

Use the table at the right for Exercises **7–9.**

7. Which desert accumulates the least amount of rain in August?

____

Average Desert Rainfall in August

Desert	Average Rainfall
Reno	0.19 mm
Sahara	0.17 mm
Mojave	0.1 mm
Tempe	0.24 mm

8. If each month in Reno had the same average rainfall as in August, what would the total number of millimeters be after 12 months?

____

9. Explain It In December, the average total rainfall in all of the deserts together is 0.89 mm. Explain how to use the figures from the table to write a comparison of the total desert rainfall in August and December.

____

____

____

10. Algebra If $4n = 3.60$, which is the value of n?

A 0.09 **B** 0.9 **C** 9 **D** 90

Name ______________________________

Practice
7-3

Estimating the Product of a Decimal and a Whole Number

Estimate each product using rounding or compatible numbers.

1. 0.97×312 ________

2. 8.02×70 ________

3. 31.04×300 ________

4. 0.56×48 ________

5. 0.33×104 ________

6. 0.83×12 ________

7. 0.89×51 ________

8. 4.05×11 ________

9. 0.13×7 ________

10. 45.1×5 ________

11. 99.3×92 ________

12. 47.2×93 ________

13. Critical Thinking Mr. Webster works 4 days a week at his office and 1 day a week at home. The distance to Mr. Webster's office is 23.7 miles. He takes a different route home, which is 21.8 miles. When Mr. Webster works at home, he drives to the post office once a day, which is 2.3 miles from his house. Which piece of information is not important in figuring out how many miles Mr. Webster drives per week to his office?

A the number of days at the office
B the distance to his office
C the distance to the post office
D the distance from his office

14. Strategy Practice Mrs. Smith bought her three children new snowsuits for winter. Each snowsuit cost $25.99. How much did Mrs. Smith pay in all?

A $259.90 **B** $77.97 **C** $51.98 **D** $25.99

15. Explain It How can estimating be helpful before finding an actual product?

____

____

____

Name ______________________________

Multiplying Two Decimals

Find each product.

1. 3.7 × 0.3

2. 4.4 × 0.2

3. 0.61 × 6.8

4. 1.9 × 0.005

5. 0.79 × 4.3 = __________

6. 0.79 × 0.005 = __________

7. Number Sense The product of 4.7 and 6.5 equals 30.55. What is the product of 4.7 and 0.65? 4.7 and 65?

____

8. What would be the gravity in relation to Earth of a planet with 3.4 times the gravity of Mercury?

____

Relative (to Earth) Surface Gravity

Planet	Gravity
Mercury	0.39
Neptune	1.22
Jupiter	2.6

9. The gravity of Venus is 0.35 times that of Jupiter. What is the gravity of Venus in relation to Earth's gravity?

____

10. How many decimal places are in the product of a number with decimal places to the thousandths multiplied by a number with decimal places to the hundredths?

A 2 **B** 3 **C** 4 **D** 5

11. Explain It Explain how you know the number of decimal places that should be in the product when you multiply two decimal numbers together.

____

____

____

____

Name ______________________

Practice
7-5

Dividing Decimals by 10, 100, or 1,000

Find each quotient. Use mental math.

1. 86.6 ÷ 10 = ________

2. 192.5 ÷ 100 = ________

3. 1.99 ÷ 100 = ________

4. 0.87 ÷ 10 = ________

5. 228.55 ÷ 1,000 = ________

6. 0.834 ÷ 100 = ________

7. 943.35 ÷ 1,000 = ________

8. 1.25 ÷ 10 = ________

Algebra Write 10, 100, or 1,000 for each *n*.

9. 78.34 ÷ *n* = 0.7834 ________

10. 0.32 ÷ *n* = 0.032 ________

11. (75.34 − 25.34) ÷ *n* = 5 ________

12. There are 145 children taking swimming lessons at the pool. If 10 children will be assigned to each instructor, how many instructors need to be hired? ________

13. Ronald ran 534.3 mi in 100 days. If he ran an equal distance each day, how many miles did he run per day?

A 5 **B** 5.13 **C** 5.343 **D** 6.201

14. Explain It Carlos says that 17.43 ÷ 100 is the same as 174.3 × 0.01. Is he correct? Explain.

____

____

Name ______________________

Practice

7-6

Dividing a Decimal by a Whole Number

Find each quotient.

1. $13\overline{)68.9}$ **2.** $35\overline{)412.3}$ **3.** $90\overline{)14.4}$ **4.** $60\overline{)53.4}$

5. 123.08 ÷ 34 = ____________ **6.** 0.57 ÷ 30 = ____________

7. 562.86 ÷ 59 = ____________ **8.** 24.4 ÷ 80 = ____________

9. John paid $7.99 for 3 boxes of cereal. The tax was $1.69. Excluding tax, how much did John pay for each box of cereal if they all were the same price?

____

10. If a package of granola bars with 12 bars costs $3.48, how much does each granola bar cost?

A 29¢ **B** 31¢ **C** 44¢ **D** $1.00

11. Estimation 64.82 ÷ 11 is

A a little more than 6. **C** a little less than 6.

B a little more than 60. **D** a little less than 60.

12. Explain It Explain how to divide 0.12 by 8.

____

____

____

____

Name ______________________

Estimation: Decimals Divided by Whole Numbers

Estimate each quotient.

1. 73.5 ÷ 10 ______ **2.** 246.78 ÷ 83 ______ **3.** 185.7 ÷ 3 ______

4. 535.6 ÷ 35 ______ **5.** 553.9 ÷ 90 ______ **6.** 366.6 ÷ 12 ______

7. 35.6 ÷ 7 ______ **8.** 86.4 ÷ 4 ______ **9.** 270.53 ÷ 3 ______

10. 839.7 ÷ 90 ______ **11.** 93.26 ÷ 3 ______ **12.** 77.3 ÷ 11 ______

13. Joseph is saving $23 a week to buy a graphing calculator that costs $275.53. About how many weeks will it take before he can buy the calculator?

____

14. Juan works at a health food store two hours a day, three days a week. His weekly pay is $73.50. About how much does Juan make per hour?

____

15. Reasonableness Which of the following is a reasonable estimate for the operation 566.3 ÷ 63?

A about 16 **B** about 9 **C** about 4 **D** about 6

16. Explain It When would you estimate a quotient instead of finding the exact quotient?

____

____

____

____

Name ______________________

Practice
7-8

Dividing a Decimal by a Decimal

Find each quotient.

1. $0.8\overline{)1.84}$ **2.** $0.9\overline{)2.7}$ **3.** $2.5\overline{)4.75}$ **4.** $1.1\overline{)1.21}$

5. $7.1\overline{)6.39}$ **6.** $0.8\overline{)0.648}$ **7.** $1.3\overline{)10.725}$ **8.** $0.2\overline{)0.51}$

9. $0.07\overline{)0.77}$ **10.** $4.8\overline{)4.32}$ **11.** $0.7\overline{)8.4}$ **12.** $2.3\overline{)6.9}$

13. Chan paid $4.75 for trail mix that costs $2.50 a pound. How many pounds of trail mix did he buy?

____

14. Max's family car has a gas tank that holds 12.5 gallons of gas. It cost $40.62 to completely fill the tank yesterday. What was the price of gas per gallon?

____

15. Strategy Practice Strawberries cost $5.99 per pound, and bananas cost $0.59 per pound. How many pounds of bananas could you buy for the cost of one pound of strawberries?

A 101.5 pounds **B** 10.15 pounds **C** 5.99 pounds **D** .59 pounds

16. Explain It When dividing a decimal by a decimal, why is it sometimes necessary to add a zero to the right of the decimal point in the quotient?

____

____

____

____

____

Name ______________________________

Practice
7-9

Problem Solving: Multiple-Step Problems

Storewide Sale	
Jeans	$29.95 for 1 pair OR 2 pairs for $55.00
T-shirts	$9.95 for 1 OR 3 T-shirts for $25.00

Write and answer the hidden question or questions in each problem and then solve the problem. Write your answer in a complete sentence.

1. Sue bought 2 pairs of jeans and a belt that cost $6.95. The tax on the items was $5.85. Sue paid the cashier $70.00. How much money did Sue receive in change?

____

2. A recreation department purchased 12 T-shirts for day camp. The department does not have to pay sales tax. It paid with a $100.00 bill. How much change did it receive?

____

____

3. When Mrs. Johnson saw the sale, she decided to get clothes for each child in her family. She bought each of her 6 children a pair of jeans and a T-shirt. She paid $14.35 in sales tax. How much was Mrs. Johnson's total bill?

A $94.35 **B** $119.70 **C** $229.35 **D** $253.35

4. Write a Problem Write a two-step problem that contains a hidden question about buying something at the mall. Tell what the hidden question is and solve your problem. Use $8.95 somewhere in your equation. Write your answer in a complete sentence.

____

____

5. Explain It What are hidden questions and why are they important when solving multiple-step problems?

____

____

Name ______________________________

Basic Geometric Ideas

Use the diagram at the right. Name the following.

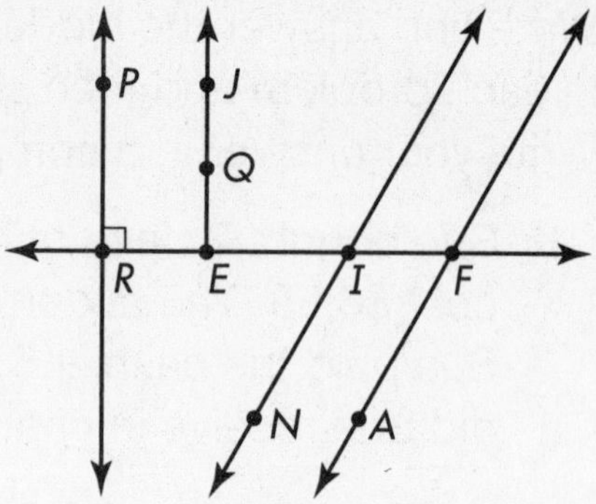

1. three points

____

2. a ray

____

3. two intersecting lines but not perpendicular

____

4. two parallel lines ______________________________

5. a line segment ______________________________

6. two perpendicular lines ______________________________

7. Explain It Can a line segment have two midpoints? Explain.

____

____

____

8. Which type of lines are shown by the figure?

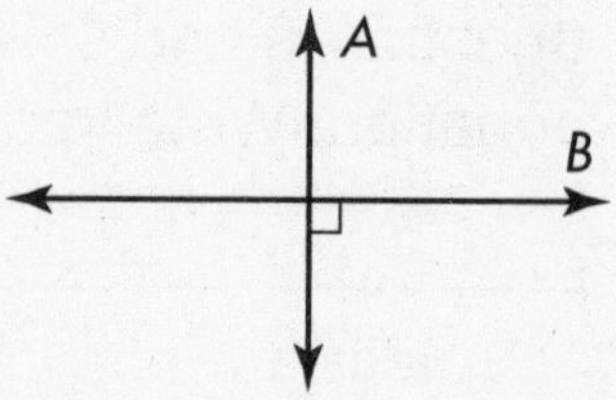

A Congruent **C** Perpendicular

B Parallel **D** Curved

9. Draw a picture Draw and label two perpendicular line segments $\overline{KL}$ and $\overline{MN}$.

Name ____________________

Practice
8-2

Measuring and Classifying Angles

Classify each angle as *acute, right, obtuse,* or *straight.* Then measure each angle. (Hint: Draw longer sides if necessary.)

1.

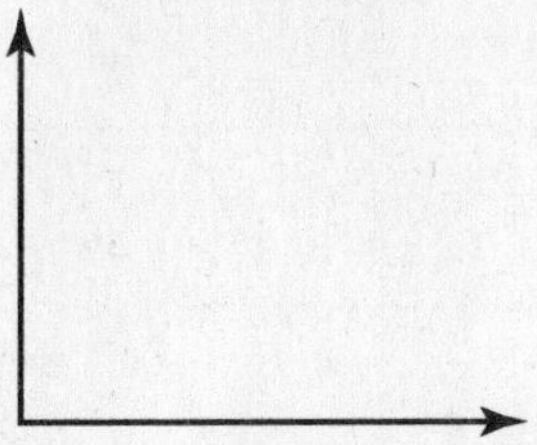

____

2.

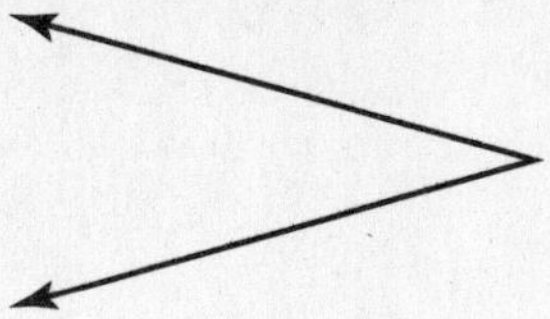

____

Draw an angle with each measure.

3. 120°

4. 180°

5. Draw an acute angle. Label it with the letters *A, B,* and *C*. What is the measure of the angle?

____

6. Which kind of angle is shown in the figure below?

A Acute

B Right

C Obtuse

D Straight

7. Explain It Explain how to use a protractor to measure an angle.

____

____

____

Name ______________________________

Polygons

Name each polygon. Then tell if it appears to be a regular polygon.

1.

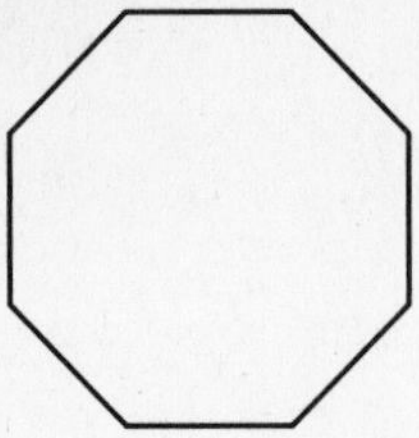

____

____

2.

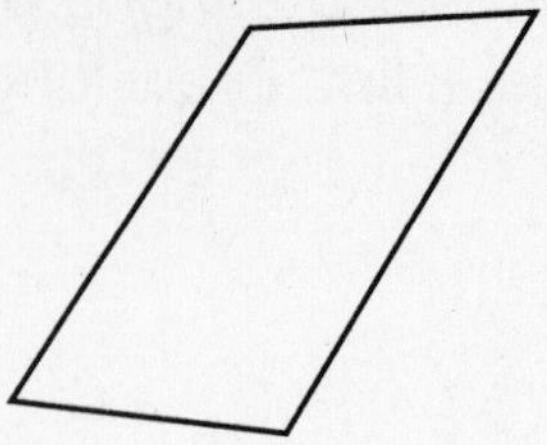

____

____

3. Name the polygon. Name the vertices.

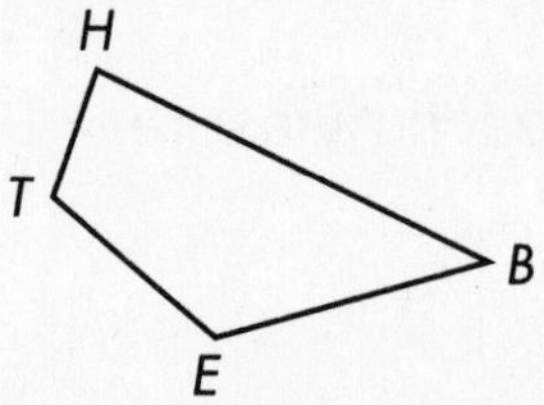

____

____

4. Which polygon has eight sides?

A quadrilateral **B** pentagon **C** hexagon **D** octagon

5. **Explain It** Draw two regular polygons and two that are irregular. Use geometric terms to describe one characteristic of each type.

____

____

____

Name ______________________________

Practice
8-4

Triangles

Classify each triangle by its sides and then by its angles.

1.

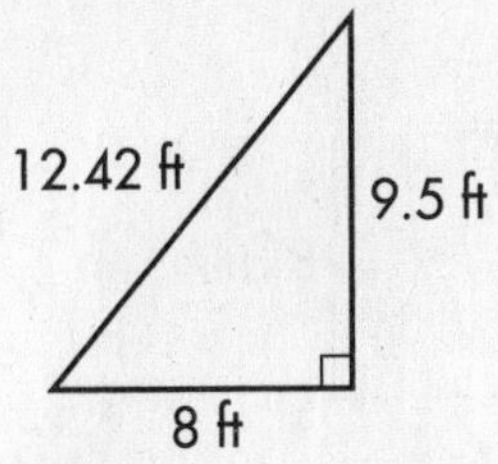

____

____

2.

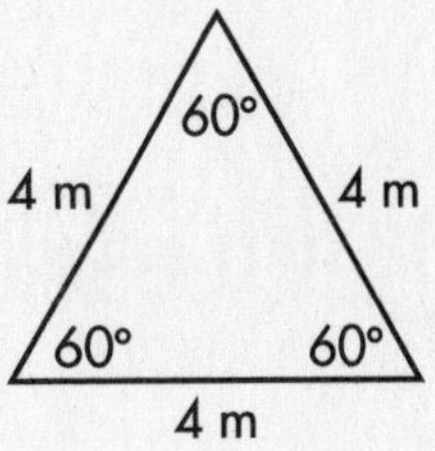

____

____

The measures of two angles of a triangle are given. Find the measure of the third angle.

3. 47°, 62°, __________

4. 29°, 90°, __________

5. 75°, 75°, __________

6. 54°, 36°, __________

7. Judy bought a new tent for a camping trip. Look at the side of the tent with the opening to classify the triangle by its sides and its angles.

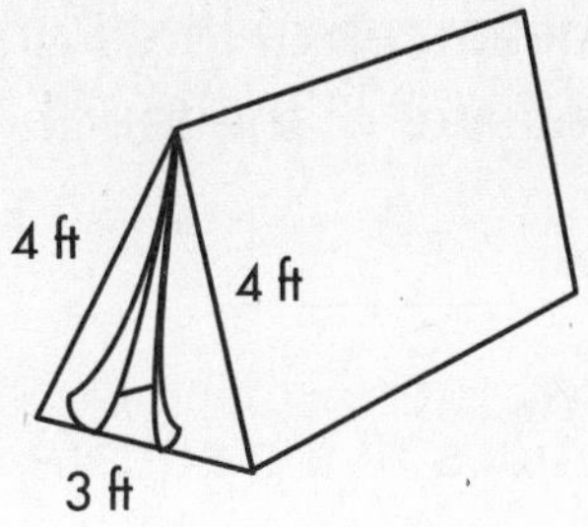

____

8. Reasonableness Which describes a scalene triangle?

A 4 equal sides **B** 3 equal sides **C** 2 equal sides **D** 0 equal sides

9. Explain It The lengths of two sides of a triangle are 15 in. each. The third side measures 10 in. What type of triangle is this? Explain your answer using geometric terms.

____

____

Name ______________________

Practice
8-5

Quadrilaterals

Classify each quadrilateral. Be as specific as possible.

1.

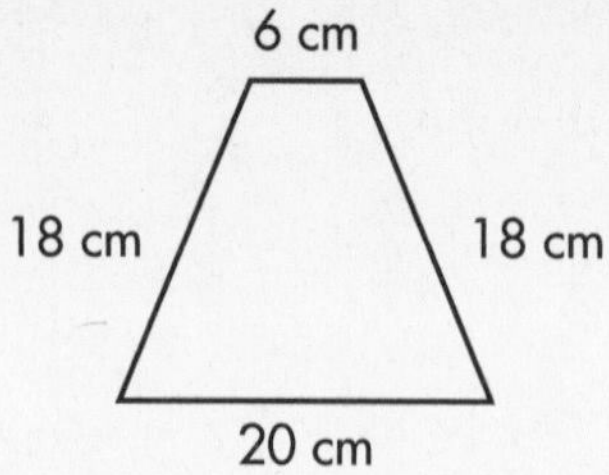

____

2.

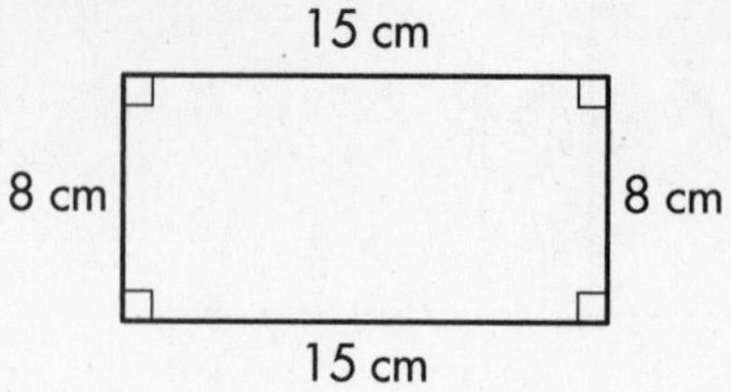

____

3.

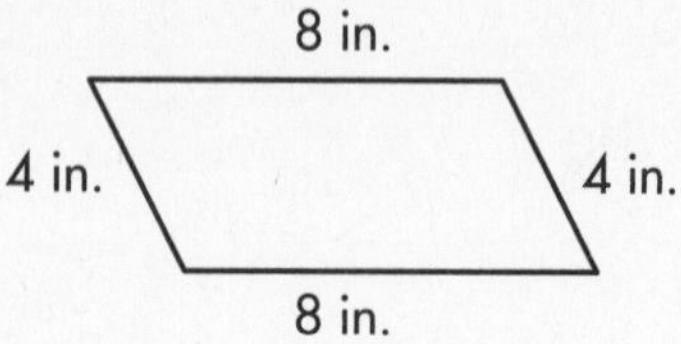

____

4.

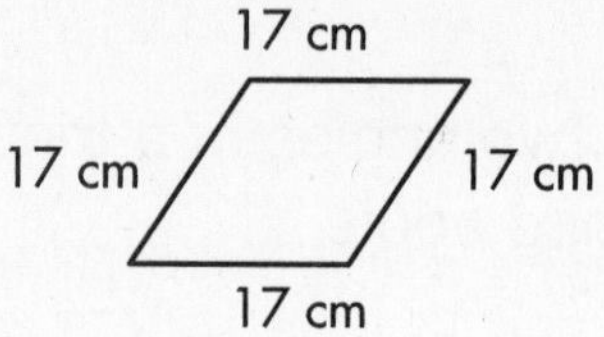

____

For **5** and **6**, the measures of three angles of a quadrilateral are given. Find the measure of the fourth angle.

5. 90°, 145°, 78°, ________

6. 110°, 54°, 100°, ________

7. Name the vertices of the square to the right.

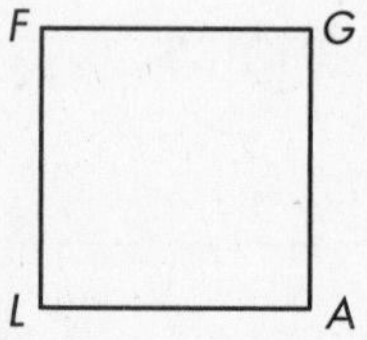

____

8. Three of the angles of a quadrilateral measure 80°, 100°, and 55°. Which is the measure of the fourth angle?

A 115° **B** 120° **C** 125° **D** 130°

9. **Explain It** Can a trapezoid have four obtuse angles? Explain.

____

____

____

Name ______________________

Practice
8-6

Problem Solving: Make and Test Generalizations

In **1** through **6**, test the generalization and state whether it appears to be correct or incorrect. If incorrect, give an example to support why.

1. All triangles have right angles.

____

2. All rectangles have right angles.

____

3. Any two triangles can be joined to make a rhombus.

____

4. All rectangles can be cut in half vertically or horizontally to make two congruent rectangles.

____

5. Intersecting lines are also parallel.

____

6. How many whole numbers have exactly three digits? Hint: 999 is the greatest whole number with three digits.

A 890 **B** 900 **C** 990 **D** 999

7. **Explain It** How can you show that a generalization is correct?

____

____

Name ______________________________

Meanings of Fractions

Write the fraction that names the shaded part.

1. 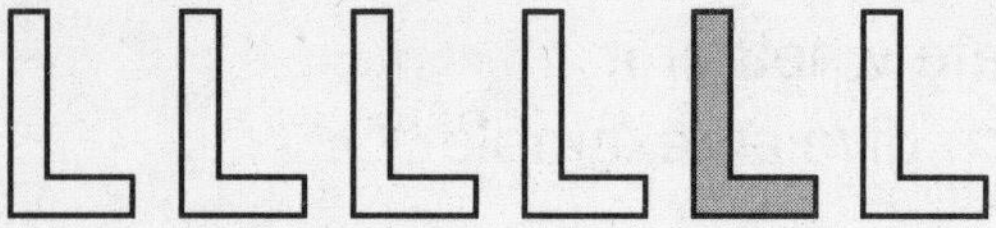 __________

2. 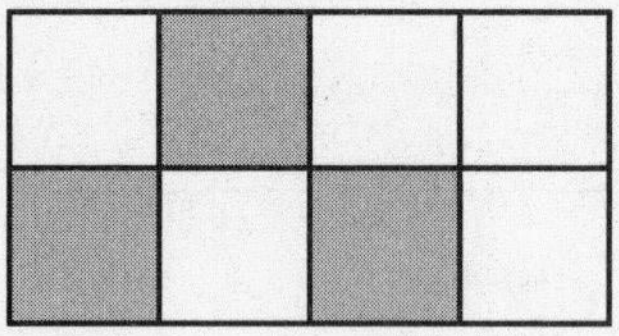 __________

In **3** and **4**, draw a model to show each fraction.

3. $\frac{4}{8}$ as part of a set

4. $\frac{5}{10}$ as part of a region

5. **Number Sense** If $\frac{5}{17}$ of a region is shaded, what part is not shaded? __________

6. Camp Big Trees has 3 red canoes and 4 blue canoes. What fraction of the canoes are red? __________

7. In a class of 24 students,13 students are girls. What fraction of the students are boys?

   A $\frac{11}{13}$ **B** $\frac{11}{24}$ **C** $\frac{13}{24}$ **D** $\frac{24}{11}$

8. **Explain It** Trisha says that if $\frac{5}{7}$ of her pencils are yellow, then $\frac{2}{7}$ are not yellow. Is she correct? Explain.

____

____

____

Name ______________________________

Practice
9-2

Fractions and Division

Give each answer as a fraction. Then graph the answer on the number line.

1. $3 \div 7$ ______

2. $4 \div 9$ ______

3. $1 \div 5$ ______

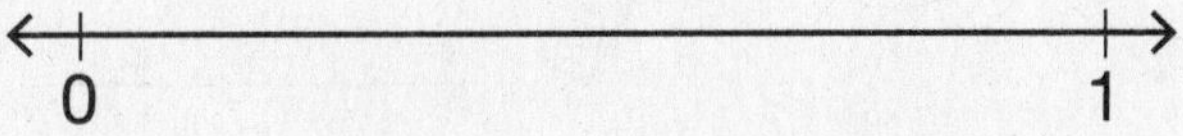

4. Use the number line to name the fraction at point *A*.

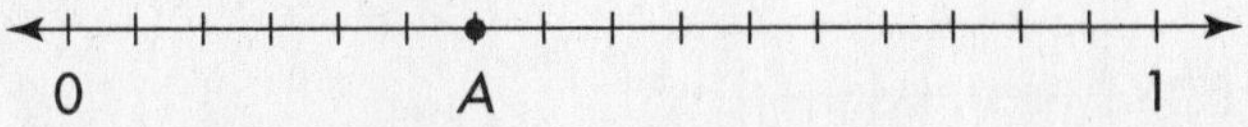

______

At a golf course, there are 18 holes. Of the 18 holes, 3 are par threes, 8 are par fours, and 7 are par fives. What fraction of the holes are

5. par fives? ______ **6.** par threes? ______ **7.** par fours? ______

8. **Number Sense** Explain how you know that $7 \div 9$ is less than 1.

____

____

9. After school, Chase spends 20 min reading, 30 min practicing the piano, 15 min cleaning his room, and 40 min doing his homework. Chase is busy for 105 min. What fraction of the time does he spend cleaning his room? ______

10. Venietta read 4 books in 7 weeks. How many books did she read each week?

A $\frac{6}{7}$ **B** $\frac{4}{7}$ **C** $\frac{3}{7}$ **D** $\frac{2}{7}$

11. **Explain It** In 5 min, Peter completed 2 math problems. Yvonne says he did $\frac{3}{5}$ of a problem each minute. Is she correct? Explain.

____

____

Name ______________________

Practice **9-3**

Mixed Numbers and Improper Fractions

Write an improper fraction and a mixed number for each model.

1. 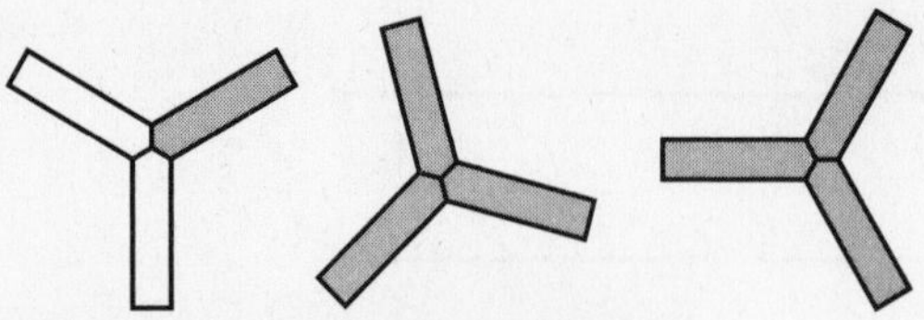 ______

2. 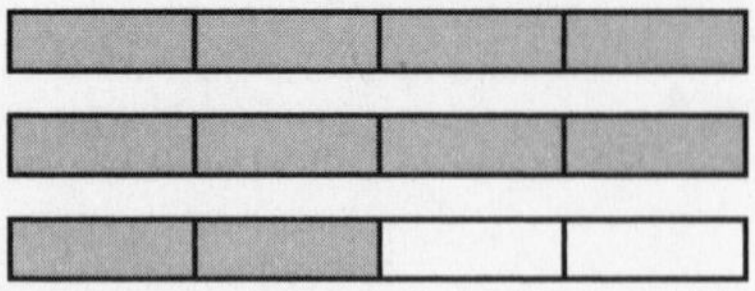 ______

Write each improper fraction as a mixed number.

3. $\frac{12}{7}$ ______ **4.** $\frac{7}{3}$ ______ **5.** $\frac{5}{2}$ ______

6. $\frac{9}{4}$ ______ **7.** $\frac{29}{13}$ ______ **8.** $\frac{34}{8}$ ______

Write each mixed number as an improper fraction.

9. $2\frac{4}{5}$ ______ **10.** $8\frac{7}{9}$ ______ **11.** $3\frac{6}{7}$ ______

12. $7\frac{1}{8}$ ______ **13.** $4\frac{3}{7}$ ______ **14.** $5\frac{1}{4}$ ______

15. Number Sense Jasmine has 41 lb of dog food to pour into 5 dishes. How many pounds of dog food should she pour in each dish?

A $4\frac{1}{5}$ lb **B** $8\frac{1}{5}$ lb **C** 10 lb **D** $11\frac{1}{8}$ lb

16. Explain It Hank needs 3 quarters to play one video game each time. If he has 14 quarters, how many times can he play? Explain.

____

____

____

____

Name ______________________

Practice 9-4

Equivalent Fractions

Name two equivalent fractions for each fraction.

1. $\frac{5}{15}$ ______

2. $\frac{6}{36}$ ______

3. $\frac{2}{12}$ ______

4. $\frac{4}{28}$ ______

5. $\frac{3}{21}$ ______

6. $\frac{2}{11}$ ______

Find the missing number to make the fractions equivalent.

7. $\frac{4}{13} = \frac{8}{x}$ ______________

8. $\frac{12}{30} = \frac{n}{90}$ ______________

9. $\frac{q}{54} = \frac{2}{9}$ ______________

10. $\frac{14}{h} = \frac{7}{20}$ ______________

11. Renie gave each of six people $\frac{1}{10}$ of a veggie pizza. Renie has $\frac{2}{5}$ of the pizza left. Explain how this is true.

____

____

12. Which fraction is equivalent to $\frac{3}{7}$?

A $\frac{3}{6}$ **B** $\frac{6}{14}$ **C** $\frac{3}{17}$ **D** $\frac{7}{7}$

13. **Explain It** Jacqueline had four $5 bills. She bought a shirt for $10. Explain what fraction of her money Jacqueline has left. Use equivalent fractions.

____

____

____

Name ________________________________

Practice **9-5**

Comparing and Ordering Fractions and Mixed Numbers

Compare the numbers. Write >, <, or = for each ◯.

1. $\frac{6}{7}$ ◯ $\frac{6}{8}$

2. $\frac{4}{9}$ ◯ $\frac{2}{3}$

3. $1\frac{1}{10}$ ◯ $1\frac{1}{12}$

4. $2\frac{4}{5}$ ◯ $2\frac{5}{6}$

5. $3\frac{6}{9}$ ◯ $3\frac{2}{3}$

6. $\frac{2}{5}$ ◯ $\frac{2}{8}$

Order the numbers from least to greatest.

7. $\frac{4}{6}, \frac{4}{8}, \frac{3}{4}, \frac{5}{8}$ ____________________

8. $4\frac{1}{4}, 4\frac{1}{8}, 5\frac{10}{11}, 4\frac{2}{12}$ ____________________

9. $1\frac{3}{7}, 1\frac{3}{4}, 1\frac{2}{4}, 1\frac{8}{14}$ ____________________

10. Number Sense How do you know that $5\frac{1}{4}$ is less than $5\frac{4}{10}$?

____

____

11. A mechanic uses four wrenches to fix Mrs. Aaron's car. The wrenches are different sizes: $\frac{5}{16}$ in., $\frac{1}{2}$ in., $\frac{1}{4}$ in., and $\frac{7}{16}$ in. Order the sizes of the wrenches from greatest to least.

____

12. Which is greater than $6\frac{1}{3}$?

A $6\frac{1}{6}$ **B** $6\frac{1}{5}$ **C** $6\frac{1}{4}$ **D** $6\frac{1}{2}$

13. Explain It Compare $3\frac{3}{22}$ and $3\frac{2}{33}$. Which is greater? How do you know?

____

____

Name ______________________

Common Factors and Greatest Common Factor

Find the GCF of each pair of numbers.

1. 15, 50 ________ **2.** 6, 27 ________ **3.** 10, 25 ________

4. 18, 32 ________ **5.** 7, 28 ________ **6.** 54, 108 ________

7. 25, 55 ________ **8.** 14, 48 ________ **9.** 81, 135 ________

10. Number Sense Can the GCF of 16 and 42 be less than 16? Explain.

____

____

____

11. A restaurant received a shipment of 42 gal of orange juice and 18 gal of cranberry juice. The juice needs to be poured into equal-sized containers. What is the largest amount of juice that each container can hold of each kind of juice? ________

12. At a day camp, there are 56 girls and 42 boys. The campers need to be split into equal groups. Each has either all girls or all boys. What is the greatest number of campers each group can have? ________

13. Which is the GCF of 24 and 64?

A 4 **B** 8 **C** 14 **D** 12

14. Explain It Do all even numbers have 2 as a factor? Explain.

____

____

Name ______________________________

Practice **9-7**

Fractions in Simplest Form

Write each fraction in simplest form.

1. $\frac{5}{10}$ ____ **2.** $\frac{6}{24}$ ____ **3.** $\frac{9}{27}$ ____

4. $\frac{3}{15}$ ____ **5.** $\frac{10}{12}$ ____ **6.** $\frac{9}{15}$ ____

7. $\frac{2}{18}$ ____ **8.** $\frac{25}{60}$ ____ **9.** $\frac{12}{72}$ ____

10. Number Sense Explain how you can tell $\frac{4}{5}$ is in simplest form.

____

____

____

Write in simplest form.

Math Test
➡ 20 Multiple-choice problems
➡ 10 Fill in the blanks
➡ 5 Word problems

11. What fraction of the problems on the math test will be word problems?

____

12. What fraction of the problems on the math test will be multiple-choice problems? ________

13. Which is the simplest form of $\frac{10}{82}$?

A $\frac{1}{8}$ **B** $\frac{1}{22}$ **C** $\frac{10}{82}$ **D** $\frac{5}{41}$

14. Explain It Explain how you can find the simplest form of $\frac{100}{1{,}000}$.

____

____

____

Name ______________________________

Practice **9-10**

Fractions and Decimals on the Number Line

Draw a number line to show the set of numbers. Then order the numbers from least to greatest.

1. 0.75, $\frac{8}{10}$, 0.2, $\frac{2}{5}$ ______________________________

Write a fraction or mixed number in simplest form and a decimal that name each point.

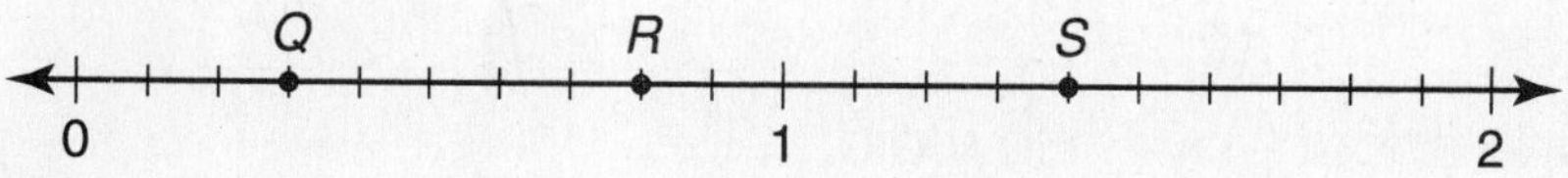

2. Point Q __________ **3.** Point R __________ **4.** Point S __________

5. Uma recorded the distances that volunteers walked in the charity event. Grace walked $1\frac{3}{5}$ mi, Wendell walked 1.3 mi, and Simon walked $1\frac{1}{10}$ mi. Show these distances on a number line. Who walked the farthest? __________

6. **Number Sense** Which is a decimal that could go between the mixed numbers $4\frac{3}{5}$ and $4\frac{9}{10}$ on a number line?

A 4.45 **B** 4.5 **C** 4.75 **D** 4.92

7. **Explain It** Explain how you know that 5.5 is to the right of $5\frac{1}{4}$ on the number line.

____

____

Name ______________________________

Practice

9-11

Problem Solving: Writing to Explain

Estimate the fractional part of the shaded portions below. Explain how you decided.

1. 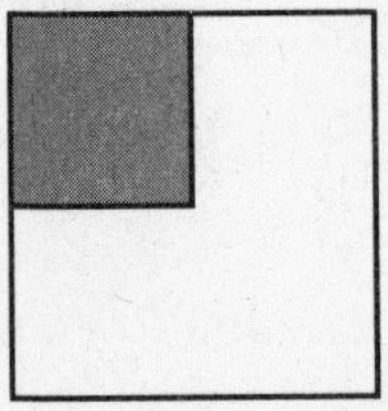

2. 

3. Draw a square and shade about $\frac{1}{8}$ of it. How did you decide how much to shade?

4. Draw two rectangles that are different sizes. Shade about $\frac{1}{2}$ of each. Are the shaded parts the same amount? Explain.

5. **Explain It** Look at a picture of the American flag. Approximately what part of the flag is blue? Explain.

Name ____________________

Practice
10-1

Adding and Subtracting Fractions with Like Denominators

Add or subtract. Simplify if possible.

1. $\frac{10}{12} + \frac{8}{12}$

2. $\frac{8}{9} - \frac{5}{9}$

3. $\frac{7}{10} + \frac{2}{10}$

4. $\frac{2}{3} - \frac{1}{3}$

5. $\frac{6}{8} + \frac{5}{8} + \frac{3}{8} =$ ____________________

6. $\frac{8}{10} - \frac{3}{10} =$ ____________________

7. $\frac{1}{4} + \frac{2}{4} + \frac{3}{4} =$ ____________________

8. $\frac{9}{11} - \frac{1}{11} =$ ____________________

9. $\frac{2}{5} + \frac{2}{5} + \frac{3}{5} =$ ____________________

10. $\frac{7}{8} - \frac{3}{8} =$ ____________________

11. What fraction could you add to $\frac{4}{7}$ to get a sum greater than 1?

____

12. Reasoning Write three fractions, using 10 as the denominator, whose sum is 1.

____

13. Which of the following represents the difference between two equal fractions?

A 1 **B** $\frac{1}{2}$ **C** $\frac{1}{4}$ **D** 0

14. Explain It In one night, George reads 3 chapters of a book with 27 chapters. After the second night, he has read a total of $\frac{8}{27}$ of the book. Explain how you would determine the number of chapters George read the second night. Solve the problem.

____

____

Name ____________________

Practice
10-2

Common Multiples and Least Common Multiple

Find the LCM of each pair of numbers.

1. 3 and 6 ________ **2.** 7 and 10 ________

3. 8 and 12 ________ **4.** 2 and 5 ________

5. 4 and 6 ________ **6.** 3 and 4 ________

7. 5 and 8 ________ **8.** 2 and 9 ________

9. 6 and 7 ________ **10.** 4 and 7 ________

11. 5 and 20 ________ **12.** 6 and 12 ________

13. Rosario is buying pens for school. Blue pens are sold in packages of 6. Black pens are sold in packages of 3, and green pens are sold in packages of 2. What is the least number of pens she can buy to have equal numbers of pens in each color?

____

14. Jason's birthday party punch calls for equal amounts of pineapple juice and orange juice. Pineapple juice comes in 6-oz cans and orange juice comes in 10-oz cans. What is the least amount he can mix of each kind of juice without having any left over?

____

15. Reasonableness Dawn ordered 4 pizzas each costing between 8 and 12 dollars. What is a reasonable total cost of all 4 pizzas?

A less than $24 **C** between $32 and $48

B between $12 and $24 **D** about $70

16. Explain It Why is 35 the LCM of 7 and 5?

____

____

Name ______________________

Practice
10-3

Adding Fractions with Unlike Denominators

Find each sum. Simplify if necessary.

1. $\frac{2}{9} + \frac{1}{3}$ ________ **2.** $\frac{1}{7} + \frac{3}{21}$ ________ **3.** $\frac{2}{3} + \frac{1}{5}$ ________

4. $\frac{1}{4} + \frac{2}{3}$ ________ **5.** $\frac{1}{12} + \frac{4}{6}$ ________ **6.** $\frac{1}{2} + \frac{3}{5}$ ________

7. $\frac{1}{6} + \frac{5}{12}$ ________ **8.** $\frac{4}{6} + \frac{1}{3}$ ________ **9.** $\frac{2}{5} + \frac{1}{8}$ ________

10. $\frac{3}{4} + \frac{4}{5}$ ________ **11.** $\frac{11}{12} + \frac{1}{3}$ ________ **12.** $\frac{4}{8} + \frac{1}{2}$ ________

Jeremy collected nickels for one week. He is making stacks of his nickels to determine how many he has. The thickness of one nickel is $\frac{1}{16}$ in.

13. How tall is a stack of 16 nickels?

____

14. What is the combined height of 3 nickels, 2 nickels, and 1 nickel?

____

15. Number Sense Which fraction is greatest?

A $\frac{5}{6}$ **B** $\frac{7}{9}$ **C** $\frac{2}{3}$ **D** $\frac{9}{12}$

16. Explain It Which equivalent fraction would you have to use in order to add $\frac{3}{5}$ to $\frac{21}{25}$?

____

Name ______________________

Practice **10-4**

Subtracting Fractions with Unlike Denominators

Find the difference. Simplify if necessary.

1. $\frac{10}{12} - \frac{1}{4}$ ______
2. $\frac{9}{10} - \frac{3}{5}$ ______
3. $\frac{7}{8} - \frac{2}{6}$ ______
4. $\frac{7}{12} - \frac{1}{4}$ ______
5. $\frac{4}{5} - \frac{1}{3}$ ______
6. $\frac{2}{3} - \frac{1}{6}$ ______
7. $\frac{4}{8} - \frac{1}{4}$ ______
8. $\frac{4}{10} - \frac{1}{5}$ ______
9. $\frac{7}{9} - \frac{2}{3}$ ______
10. $\frac{9}{15} - \frac{1}{3}$ ______
11. $\frac{4}{12} - \frac{1}{6}$ ______
12. $\frac{14}{20} - \frac{3}{5}$ ______

13. The pet shop owner told Jean to fill her new fish tank $\frac{3}{4}$ full with water. Jean filled it $\frac{9}{12}$ full. What fraction of the tank does Jean still need to fill?

____

14. Paul's dad made a turkey pot pie for dinner on Wednesday. The family ate $\frac{4}{8}$ of the pie. On Thursday after school, Paul ate $\frac{2}{16}$ of the pie for a snack. What fraction of the pie remained?

____

15. **Algebra** Gracie read 150 pages of a book she got for her birthday. The book is 227 pages long. Which equation shows how to find the amount she still needs to read to finish the story?

A $150 - n = 227$

B $227 + 150 = n$

C $n - 150 = 227$

D $n + 150 = 227$

16. **Explain It** Why do fractions need to have a common denominator before you add or subtract them?

____

____

____

Name ______________________

Practice
10-5

Adding Mixed Numbers

Estimate the sum first. Then add. Simplify if necessary.

1. $7\frac{2}{3} + 8\frac{5}{6}$ ________ **2.** $4\frac{3}{4} + 2\frac{2}{5}$ ________

3. $11\frac{9}{10} + 3\frac{1}{20}$ ________ **4.** $7\frac{6}{7} + 5\frac{2}{7}$ ________

5. $5\frac{8}{9} + 3\frac{1}{2}$ ________ **6.** $21\frac{11}{12} + 17\frac{2}{3}$ ________

7. Number Sense Write two mixed numbers with a sum of 3.

____

8. What is the total measure of an average man's brain and heart in kilograms?

____

Vital Organ Measures

Average woman's brain	$1\frac{3}{10}$ kg	$2\frac{4}{5}$ lb
Average man's brain	$1\frac{2}{5}$ kg	3 lb
Average human heart	$\frac{3}{10}$ kg	$\frac{7}{10}$ lb

9. What is the total weight of an average woman's brain and heart in pounds? ________________

10. What is the sum of the measures of an average man's brain and an average woman's brain in kilograms? ________________

11. Which is a good comparison of the estimated sum and the actual sum of $7\frac{7}{8} + 2\frac{11}{12}$?

A Estimated $<$ actual

B Actual $=$ estimated

C Actual $>$ estimated

D Estimated $>$ actual

12. Explain It Can the sum of two mixed numbers be equal to 2? Explain why or why not.

____

____

____

Name ______________________

Practice
10-6

Subtracting Mixed Numbers

Estimate the difference first. Then subtract. Simplify if necessary.

1. $10\frac{3}{4} - 7\frac{1}{4}$ ______

2. $7\frac{3}{7} - 2\frac{8}{21}$ ______

3. $3 - 2\frac{2}{3}$ ______

4. $17\frac{7}{8} - 12\frac{3}{12}$ ______

5. $9\frac{5}{9} - 6\frac{5}{6}$ ______

6. $4\frac{3}{4} - 2\frac{2}{3}$ ______

7. $6\frac{1}{4} - 3\frac{1}{3}$ ______

8. $5\frac{1}{5} - 3\frac{7}{8}$ ______

9. $8\frac{2}{7} - 7\frac{1}{3}$ ______

10. $2\frac{9}{10} - 2\frac{1}{3}$ ______

Strategy Practice The table shows the length and width of several kinds of bird eggs.

Egg Sizes

Bird	Length	Width
Canada goose	$3\frac{2}{5}$ in.	$2\frac{3}{10}$ in.
Robin	$\frac{3}{4}$ in.	$\frac{3}{5}$ in.
Turtledove	$1\frac{1}{5}$ in.	$\frac{9}{10}$ in.
Raven	$1\frac{9}{10}$ in.	$1\frac{3}{10}$ in.

11. How much longer is the Canada goose egg than the raven egg?

______

12. How much wider is the turtledove egg than the robin egg?

______

13. Which is the difference of $21\frac{15}{16} - 18\frac{3}{4}$?

A $2\frac{7}{16}$ **B** $2\frac{9}{16}$ **C** $3\frac{3}{16}$ **D** $3\frac{9}{16}$

14. Explain It Explain why it is necessary to rename $4\frac{1}{4}$ if you subtract $\frac{3}{4}$ from it.

____

____

____

Name ____________________

Practice
10-7

Problem Solving: Try, Check, and Revise

For questions **1** and **2**, suppose you have 2 × 2 ft, 3 × 3 ft, 4 × 4 ft, and 5 × 5 ft tiles.

1. Which tiles can be used to cover a 12 × 12 ft floor? ____________________

2. Which tiles can be used to cover a 9 × 9 ft floor? ____________________

3. What size rectangular floor can be completely covered by using only 3 × 3 ft tiles OR 5 × 5 ft tiles? Remember, you can't cut tiles or combine the two tile sizes.

____

4. Adult tickets cost $6 and children's tickets cost $4. Mrs. LeCompte says that she paid $30 for tickets, for both adults and children. How many of each ticket did she buy?

____

____

5. **Reasoning** The sum of two odd numbers is 42. They are both prime numbers, and the difference of the two numbers is 16. What are the two numbers?

A 20 and 22

B 17 and 25

C 9 and 33

D 13 and 29

6. **Explain It** Marcy wants to put tiles on a bathroom floor that measures 10 ft × 12 ft. What kind of square tiles should she buy to tile her floor? Explain.

____

____

Name ______________________

Practice 11-1

Multiplying Fractions and Whole Numbers

Find each product.

1. $\frac{1}{4}$ of 96 = ______

2. $\frac{4}{7}$ of 28 = ______

3. $\frac{3}{4} \times 72$ = ______

4. $45 \times \frac{3}{9}$ = ______

5. $56 \times \frac{7}{8}$ = ______

6. $42 \times \frac{3}{7}$ = ______

7. $\frac{1}{2}$ of 118 = ______

8. $\frac{3}{8}$ of 56 = ______

9. $\frac{1}{10} \times 400$ = ______

10. $84 \times \frac{1}{6}$ = ______

11. $64 \times \frac{5}{16}$ = ______

12. $40 \times \frac{11}{20}$ = ______

13. $\frac{5}{8}$ of 48 = ______

14. $\frac{1}{7}$ of 77 = ______

15. $\frac{4}{5} \times 90$ = ______

16. $42 \times \frac{3}{14}$ = ______

17. $72 \times \frac{5}{8}$ = ______

18. $18 \times \frac{2}{3}$ = ______

19. $\frac{5}{6} \times 84$ = ______

20. $\frac{11}{12} \times 144$ = ______

21. $\frac{6}{7} \times 42$ = ______

22. Strategy Practice Complete the table by writing the product of each expression in the box below it. Use a pattern to find each product. Explain the pattern.

$\frac{1}{2} \times 32$	$\frac{1}{4} \times 32$	$\frac{1}{8} \times 32$	$\frac{1}{16} \times 32$

____

23. Reasoning If $\frac{1}{2}$ of 1 is $\frac{1}{2}$, what is $\frac{1}{2}$ of 2, 3, and 4? ______________

24. Which is $\frac{2}{3}$ of 225?

A 75 **B** 113 **C** 150 **D** 450

25. Explain It Explain why $\frac{1}{2}$ of 2 equals one whole.

____

____

Name ______________________________

Practice
11-2

Multiplying Two Fractions

Write the multiplication problem that each model represents then solve. Put your answer in simplest form.

1. 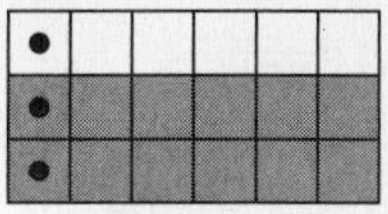

____

2. 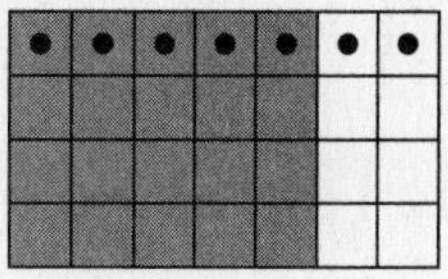

____

Find each product. Simplify if possible.

3. $\frac{7}{8} \times \frac{4}{5} =$ ____________

4. $\frac{3}{7} \times \frac{2}{3} =$ ____________

5. $\frac{1}{6} \times \frac{2}{5} =$ ____________

6. $\frac{2}{7} \times \frac{1}{4} =$ ____________

7. $\frac{2}{9} \times \frac{1}{2} =$ ____________

8. $\frac{3}{4} \times \frac{1}{3} =$ ____________

9. $\frac{3}{8} \times \frac{4}{9} =$ ____________

10. $\frac{1}{5} \times \frac{5}{6} =$ ____________

11. $\frac{2}{3} \times \frac{5}{6} \times 14 =$ ____________

12. $\frac{1}{2} \times \frac{1}{3} \times \frac{1}{4} =$ ____________

13. Algebra If $\frac{4}{5} \times \blacksquare = \frac{2}{5}$, what is $\blacksquare$? ____________

14. Ms. Shoemaker's classroom has 35 desks arranged in 5 by 7 rows. How many students does Ms. Shoemaker have in her class if there are $\frac{6}{7} \times \frac{4}{5}$ desks occupied? ____________

15. Which does the model represent?

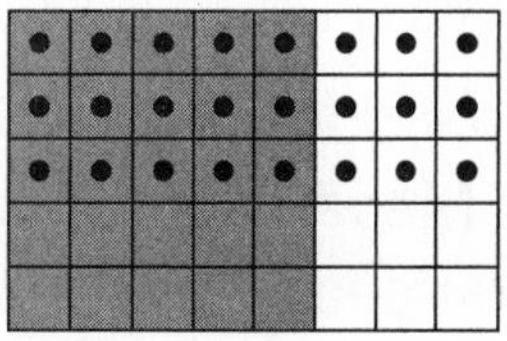

A $\frac{3}{8} \times \frac{3}{5}$

B $\frac{7}{8} \times \frac{2}{5}$

C $\frac{3}{5} \times \frac{5}{8}$

D $\frac{4}{8} \times \frac{3}{5}$

16. Explain It Describe a model that represents $\frac{3}{3} \times \frac{4}{4}$.

____

____

Name ______________________________

Practice
11-3

Multiplying Mixed Numbers

Estimate the product. Then complete the multiplication.

1. $5\frac{4}{5} \times 7 = \frac{\square}{5} \times \frac{7}{1} = \square$

2. $3\frac{2}{3} \times 5\frac{1}{7} = \frac{\square}{3} \times \frac{\square}{7} = \square$

Estimate. Then find each product. Simplify.

3. $4\frac{3}{5} \times \frac{2}{3}$ ______________

4. $6 \times 2\frac{2}{7}$ ______________

5. $7\frac{4}{5} \times 2\frac{1}{3}$ ______________

6. $3\frac{3}{4} \times 2\frac{4}{5}$ ______________

7. $2\frac{1}{5} \times \frac{7}{8}$ ______________

8. $6\frac{1}{3} \times 1\frac{5}{6}$ ______________

9. $1\frac{4}{5} \times 1\frac{1}{3} \times 1\frac{3}{4}$ ______________

10. $\frac{3}{4} \times 2\frac{2}{3} \times 5\frac{1}{5}$ ______________

11. **Algebra** Write a mixed number for p so that $3\frac{1}{4} \times p$ is more than $3\frac{1}{4}$.

____

12. A model house is built on a base that measures $9\frac{1}{4}$ in. wide and $8\frac{4}{5}$ in. long. What is the total area of the model house's base?

____

13. Which is $1\frac{3}{4}$ of $150\frac{1}{2}$?

A 263 **B** $263\frac{1}{8}$ **C** $263\frac{3}{8}$ **D** $264\frac{3}{8}$

14. **Explain It** Megan's dog Sparky eats $4\frac{1}{4}$ cups of food each day. Explain how Megan can determine how much food to give Sparky if she needs to feed him only $\frac{2}{3}$ as much. Solve the problem.

____

____

Name ______________________

Relating Division to Multiplication of Fractions

In **1** and **2**, use the picture to find each quotient.

1. How many thirds are in 1?

____

2. How many thirds are in 7?

____

In **3** and **4**, draw a picture to find each quotient.

3. $3 \div \frac{1}{2}$

____

4. $4 \div \frac{1}{8}$

____

In **5** and **6**, use multiplication to find each quotient.

5. $6 \div \frac{1}{3}$

____

6. $5 \div \frac{1}{10}$

____

7. Julie bought 3 yards of cloth to make holiday napkin rings. If she needs $\frac{3}{4}$ of a yard to make each ring, how many rings can she make?

____

8. **Reasoning** When you divide a whole number by a fraction with a numerator of 1, explain how you can find the quotient.

____

____

____

Name ______________________________

Practice
11-5

Problem Solving: Draw a Picture and Write an Equation

Solve each problem. Draw a picture to show the main idea for each problem. Then write an equation and solve it. Write the answer in a complete sentence.

1. Bobby has 3 times as many model spaceships as his friend Sylvester does. Bobby has 21 spaceships. How many model spaceships does Sylvester have?

____

____

2. Dan saved $463 over the 12 weeks of summer break. He saved $297 of it during the last 4 weeks. How much did he save during the first 8 weeks?

____

____

3. Strategy Practice Use a separate sheet of paper to show the main idea for the following problem. Choose the answer that solves the problem correctly.

A box of peanut-butter crackers was divided evenly among 6 children. Each child got 9 crackers. How many crackers were in the box?

A 54 **B** 48 **C** 39 **D** 36

4. Explain It Why is it helpful to draw a picture when attempting to solve an equation?

____

____

Name ____________________

Practice
12-1

Using Customary Units of Length

Measure each segment to the nearest inch, $\frac{1}{2}$ inch, $\frac{1}{4}$ inch, and $\frac{1}{8}$ inch.

1. ____________________

2. ____________________

3. **Reasoning** Sarah gave the same answer when asked to round $4\frac{7}{8}$ in. to the nearest $\frac{1}{2}$ inch and the nearest inch. Explain why Sarah is correct.

____

____

4. Estimate the length of your thumb. Then use a ruler to find the actual measure.

____

5. **Estimation** A real motorcycle is 18 times as large as a model motorcycle. If the model motorcycle is $5\frac{1}{16}$ in. long, about how long is the real motorcycle?

A 23 in. **B** 48 in. **C** 90 in. **D** 112 in.

6. **Explain It** If a line is measured as $1\frac{4}{8}$ in. long, explain how you could simplify the measurement.

____

____

____

Name ______________________

Using Metric Units of Length

Measure each segment to the nearest centimeter then to the nearest millimeter.

1. |————————————————| ______________

2. |————————————| ______________

Number Sense Some of the events at an upcoming track and field meet are shown at the right.

Track and Field Events

50-m dash
1,500-m dash
400-m dash
100-m dash

3. In which event or events do athletes travel more than a kilometer?

____

4. In which event or events do athletes travel less than a kilometer?

____

5. **Reasonableness** Which unit would be most appropriate for measuring the distance from Chicago to Miami?

A mm **B** cm **C** m **D** km

6. **Explain It** List one item in your classroom you would measure using centimeters and one item in the classroom you would measure using meters.

____

____

Name ______________________

Practice
12-3

Perimeter

Find the perimeter of each figure.

1.

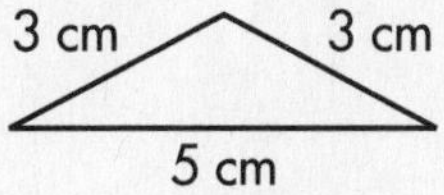

____

2.

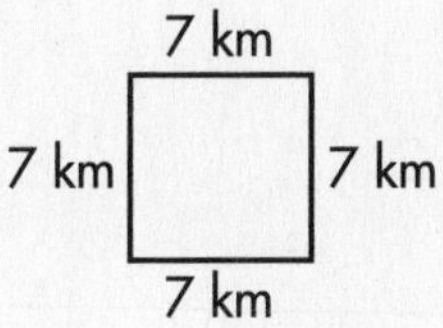

____

3.

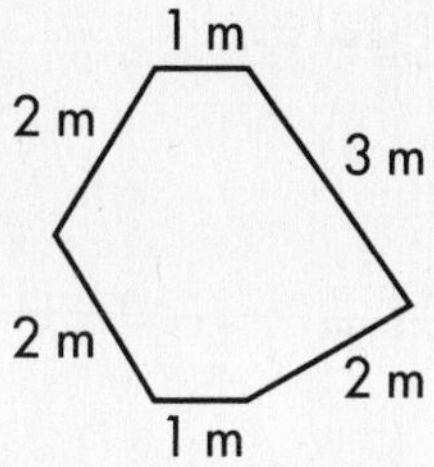

____

4.

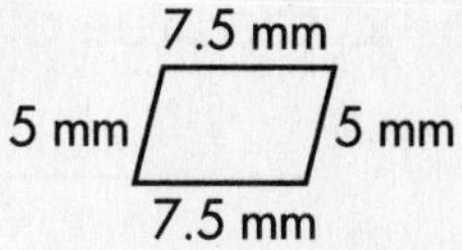

____

5. Number Sense What is the perimeter of a square if one of the sides is 3 mi? ______________

Use the dimensions of the football field shown at the right for **6** and **7**.

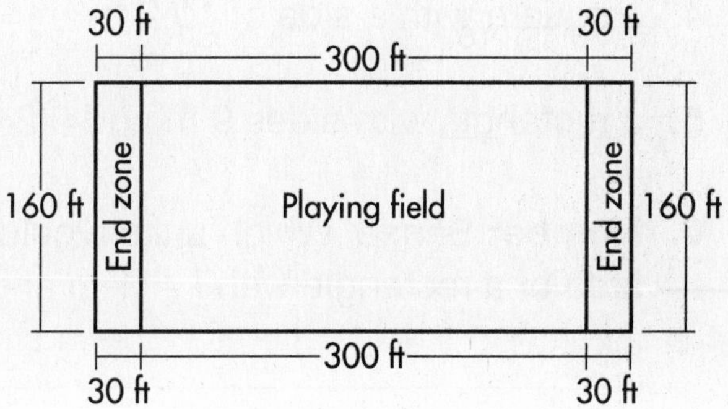

6. What is the perimeter of the entire football field including the end zones?

____

7. What is the perimeter of each end zone?

____

8. What is the perimeter of this figure?

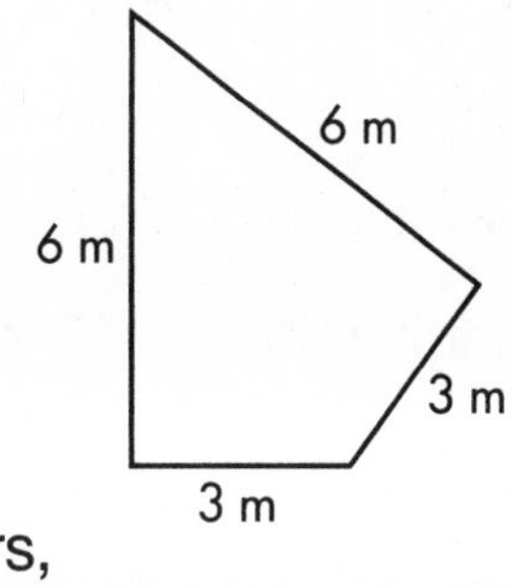

A 18 m **C** 12 m

B 15 ft **D** 10 ft

9. Explain It A rectangle has a perimeter of 12 m. If each side is a whole number of meters, what are the possible dimensions for the length and width? List them and explain your answer.

____

____

____

Name ______________________

Practice
12-4

Areas of Squares and Rectangles

Find the area of each figure.

1.

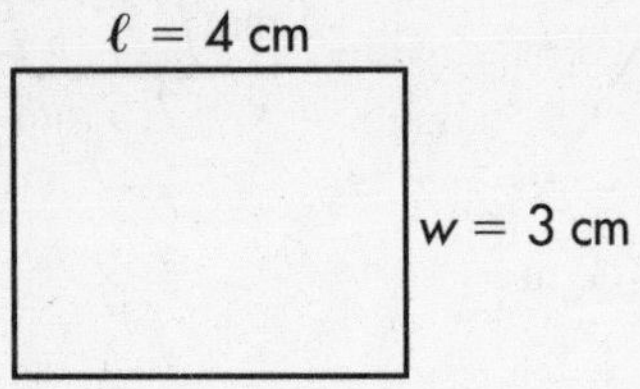

____

2.

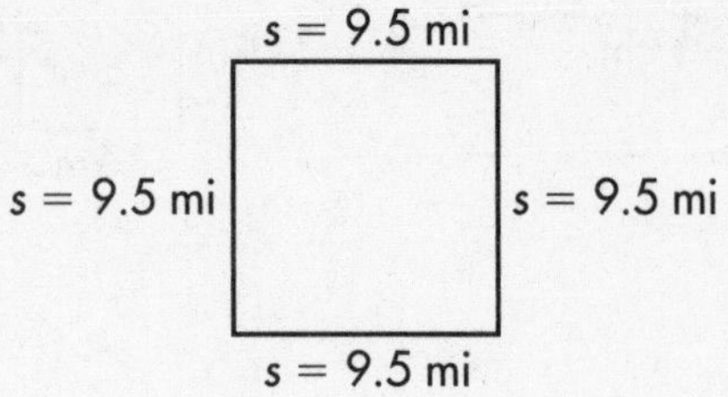

____

3. a rectangle with sides 6.5 km and 3.4 km ______________

4. a square with a side of 10.2 ft ______________

5. a rectangle with sides 9 m and 9.2 m ______________

6. Number Sense Which units would you use to measure the area of a rectangle with $l = 1$ m and $w = 34$ cm? Explain.

____

____

7. Which of the following shapes has an area of 34 ft^2?

A a square with $s = 8.5$ m

B a rectangle with $l = 15$ ft, $w = 2$ ft

C a square with $s = 16$ ft

D a rectangle with $l = 17$ ft, $w = 2$ ft

8. Explain It The area of a square is 49 m^2. What is the length of one of its sides? Explain how you solved this problem.

____

____

____

Name ______________________

Practice
12-5

Area of Parallelograms

Find the area of each parallelogram.

1.

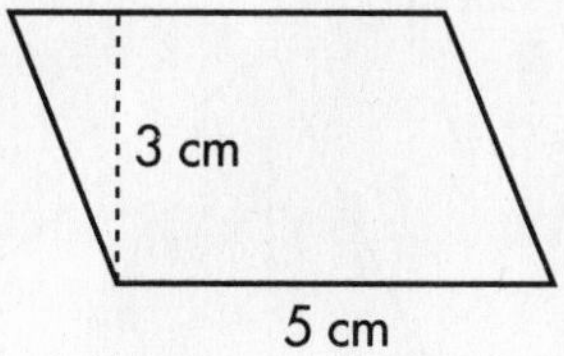

____

2.

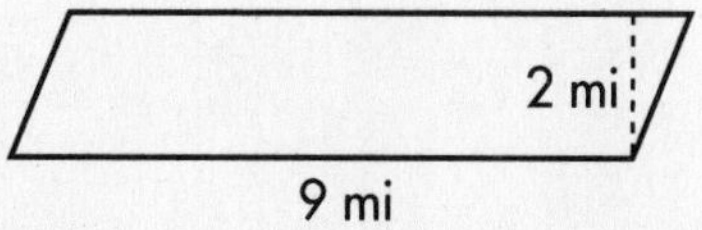

____

3.

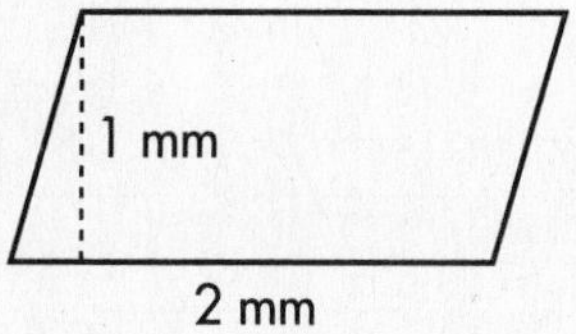

____

4.

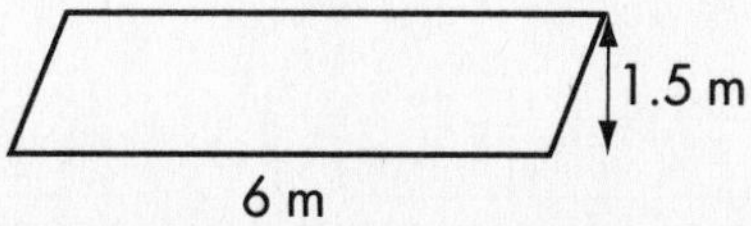

____

Algebra Find the missing measurement for the parallelogram.

5. $A = 34\text{ in}^2$, $b = 17$ in., $h =$ ______________

6. List three sets of base and height measurements for parallelograms with areas of 40 square units.

____

____

7. Which is the height of the parallelogram?

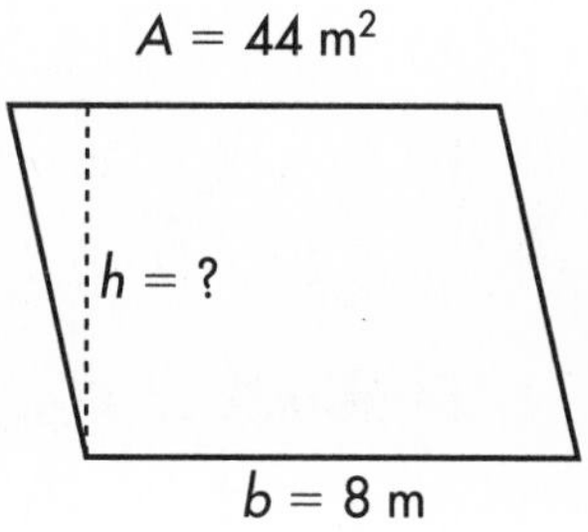

A 55 m

B 55.5 m

C 5 m

D 5.5 m

8. Explain It What are a possible base and height for a parallelogram with an area of 45 ft^2 if the base and height are a whole number of feet? Explain how you solved this problem.

____

____

Name ____________________

Practice 12-6

Area of Triangles

Find the area of each triangle.

1. 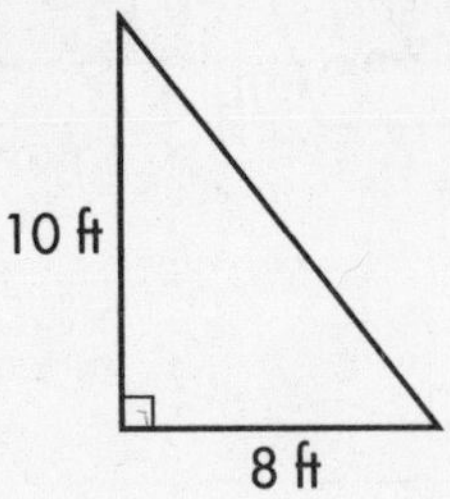

2. 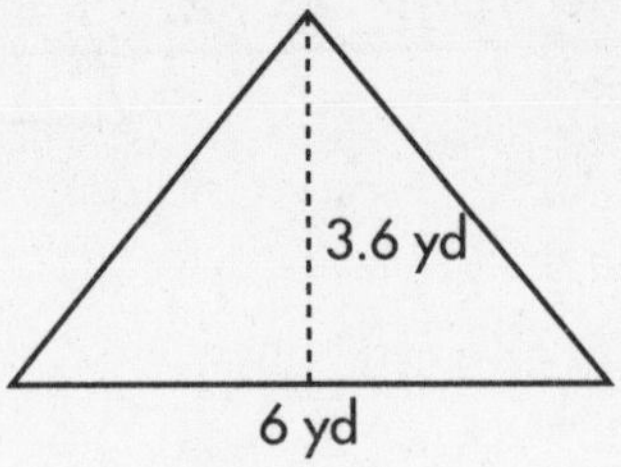

3. 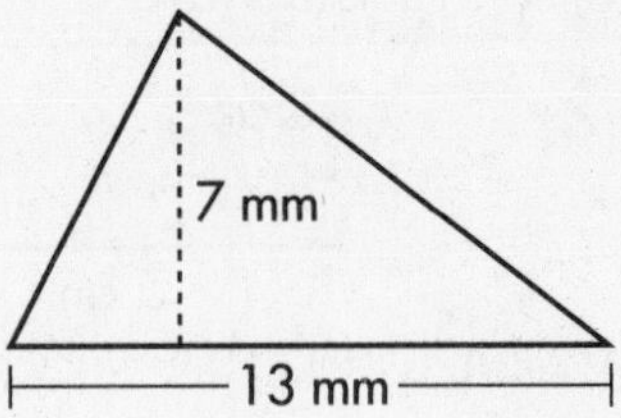

4. **Number Sense** What is the base measurement of a triangle with an area of 30 m^2 and a height of 10 m?

Algebra Find the missing measurement for each triangle.

5. $A = 36$ mi^2, $b =$ ____________, $h = 12$ mi

6. $A =$ ____________, $b = 12$ mm, $h = 7.5$ mm

7. List three sets of base and height measurements for triangles with areas of 30 square units.

8. Which is the height of the triangle?

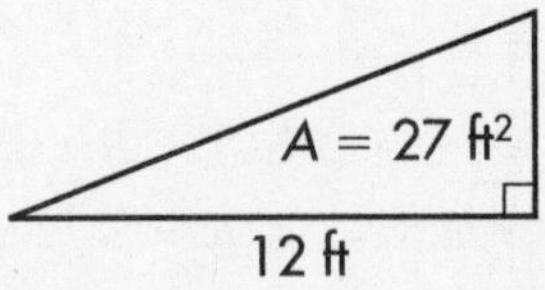

A 4.5 ft **C** 8 ft

B 6 ft **D** 9 ft

9. **Explain It** Can you find the base and height measurements for a triangle if you know that the area is 22 square units? Explain why or why not.

Name ______________________

Circles and Circumference

In **1** through **3**, use circle *X* to identify the following.

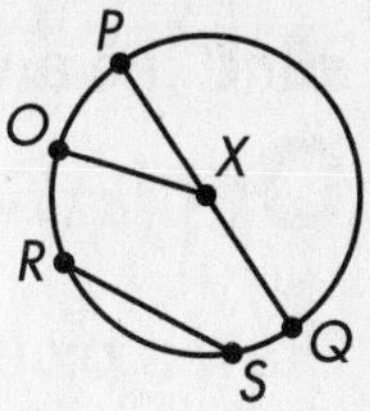

1. a diameter ______ **2.** two chords ______ **3.** a central angle ______

In **4** through **9**, find the circumference. Use 3.14 for π.

4. $d = 20$ in. ______ **5.** $d = 5$ yd ______ **6.** $d = 9$ cm ______

7. $r = 3.20$ in. ______ **8.** $r = 13$ ft ______ **9.** $r = 20$ yd ______

10. A round swimming pool has a radius of 8 meters. What is its circumference?

______

11. **Estimation** The length of the diameter of a circle is 11 centimeters. Is the circumference more or less than 33 centimeters? Explain.

______

______

12. Which equation can be used to find the circumference of a circle with a radius that measures 10 feet?

A $C = 2 \times \pi \times 20$

B $C = 2 \times \pi \times 10$

C $C = \pi \times 1.0$

D $C = \pi \times 10$

Name ____________________

Practice
12-8

Problem Solving: Draw a Picture and Make an Organized List

Draw a picture and make a list to solve.

1. Erica painted a picture of her dog. The picture has an area of 3,600 cm^2 and is square. She has placed the picture in a frame that is 5 cm wide. What is the perimeter of the picture frame?

____

2. The new playground at Middledale School will be enclosed by a fence. The playground will be rectangular and will have an area of 225 yd^2. The number of yards on each side will be a whole number. What is the least amount of fencing that could be required to enclose the playground?

____

3. **Reasoning** Evan is thinking of a 3-digit odd number that uses the digit 7 twice. The digit in the tens place is less than one. What is the number?

   A 707

   B 717

   C 770

   D 777

4. **Explain It** Explain how you solved Exercise 3.

____

____

____

Name ____________________

Practice 13-1

Solids

For **1** through **3**, use the solid at the right.

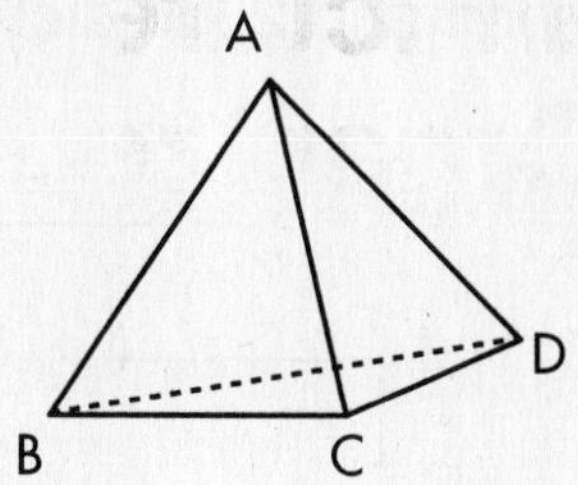

1. Name the vertices.

____

2. Name the faces.

____

____

3. Name the edges.

____

____

For **4** through **6**, tell which solid figure each object resembles.

4. 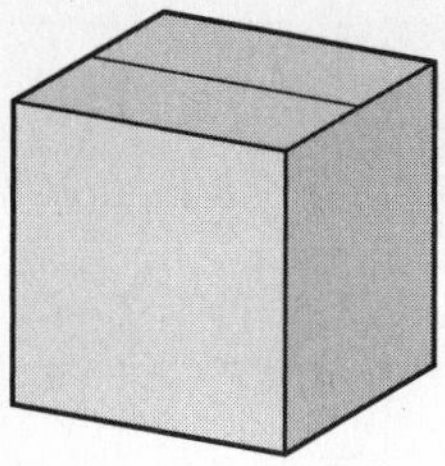

5. 

6. 

______________ ______________ ______________

7. Which term best describes the figure at the right?

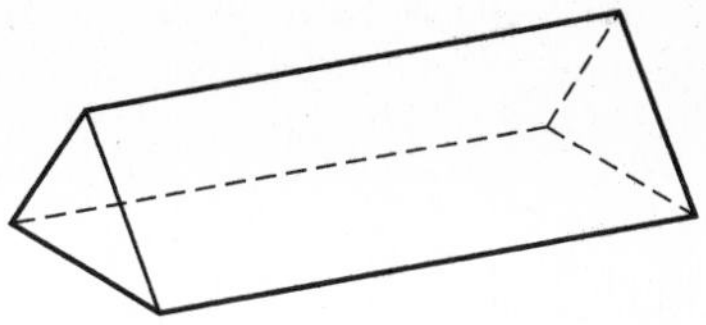

A Cone
B Triangular prism
C Pyramid
D Rectangular prism

8. Explain It How many vertices does a cone have? Explain.

____

____

Name ____________________

Practice
13-2

Relating Shapes and Solids

For **1** and **2**, predict what shape each net will make.

1.

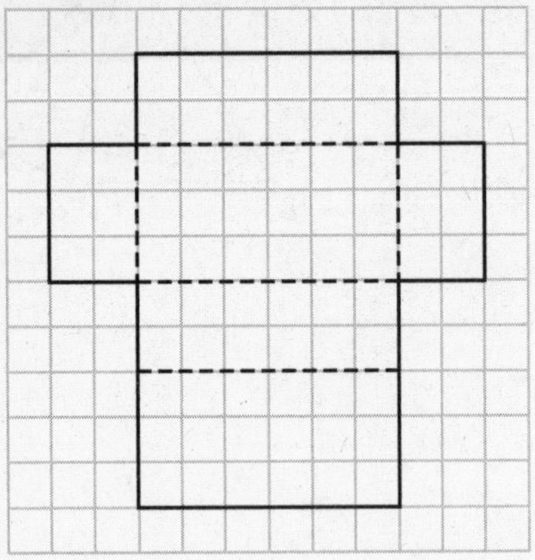

____

2.

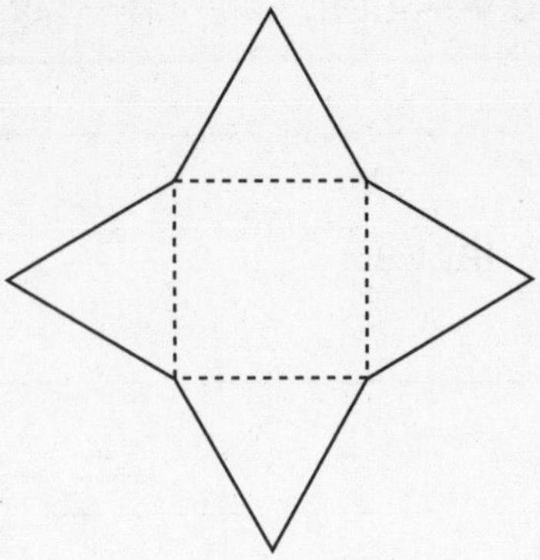

____

Reasoning For **3** through **5**, tell which solid figures could be made from the descriptions given.

3. A net that has 6 squares ____________________

4. A net that has 4 triangles ____________________

5. A net that has 2 circles and a rectangle ____________________

6. Which solid can be made by a net that has exactly one circle in it?

A Cone **B** Cylinder **C** Sphere **D** Pyramid

7. Explain It Draw a net for a triangular pyramid. Explain how you know your diagram is correct.

____

____

____

____

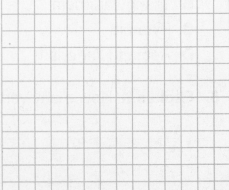

Name ____________________

Surface Area

Find the surface area of each rectangular prism.

1. 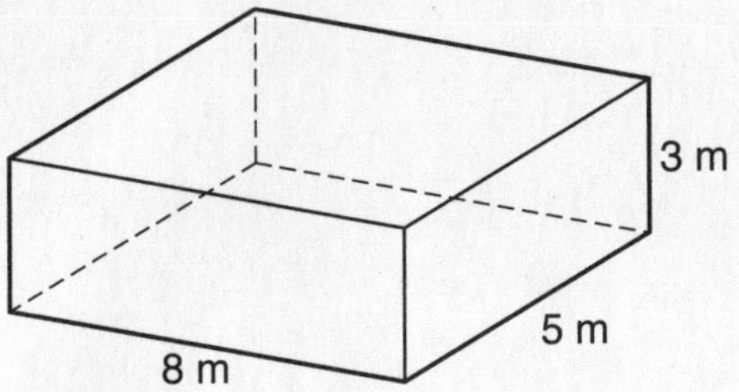

____

2. 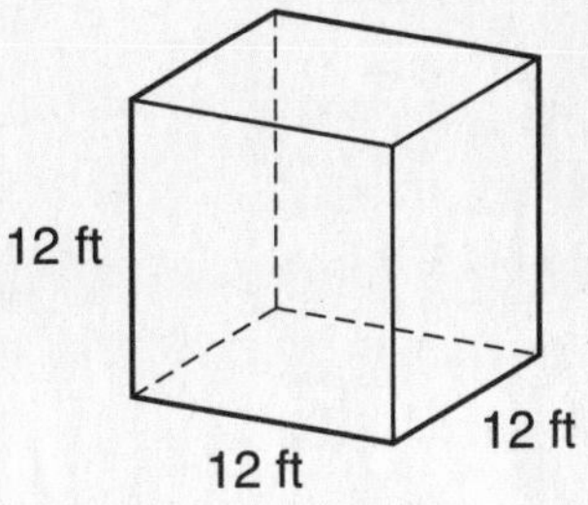

____

Strategy Practice Music and computer CDs are often stored in plastic cases called jewel cases.

3. One size of jewel case is 140 mm × 120 mm × 4 mm. What is the surface area of this jewel case?

____

4. A jewel case that holds 2 CDs is 140 mm × 120 mm × 9 mm. What is the surface area of this jewel case?

____

5. What is the surface area of a rectangular prism with the dimensions 3 in. by 4 in. by 8 in.?

A 96 in^2 **B** 112 in^2 **C** 136 in^2 **D** 152 in^2

6. **Explain It** Explain why the formula for finding the surface area of a rectangular prism is helpful.

____

____

____

Name ________________________________

Views of Solids

For **1** and **2**, draw front, side, and top views of each stack of unit blocks.

1. 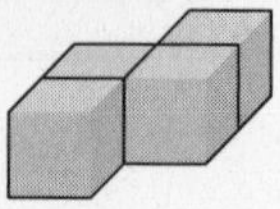

2. 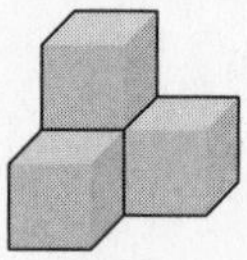

3. **Reasoning** In the figure for Exercise **2**, how many blocks are not visible?

____

4. In the figure at the right, how many unit blocks are being used?

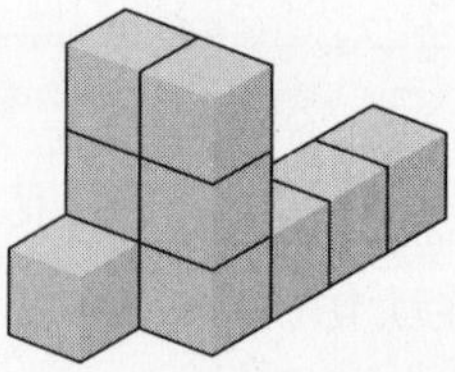

A 8

B 9

C 10

D 11

5. **Explain It** A figure is made from 8 unit blocks. It is 3 units tall. What is the maximum length the figure could be? Explain.

____

____

____

Name ______________________________

Practice
13-5

Volume

Find the volume of each rectangular prism.

1. base area 56 in.^{2}, height 6 in. ______________

2. base area 32 cm^2, height 12 cm ______________

3. base area 42 m^2, height 8 m ______________

4.

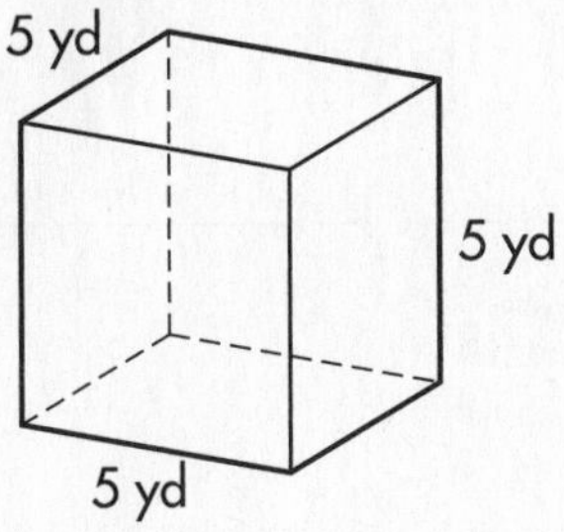

____

5.

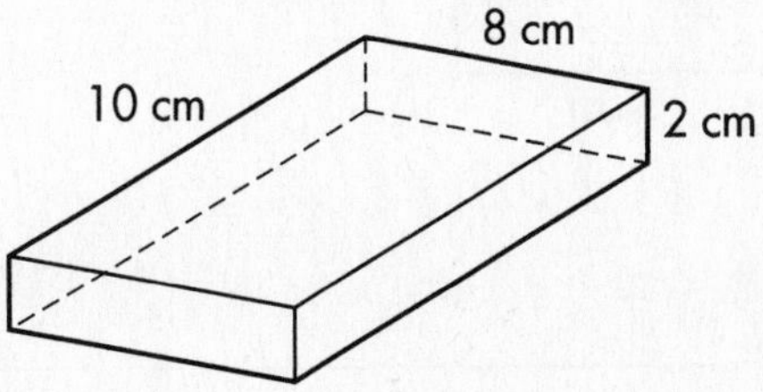

____

6. Algebra What is the height of a solid with a volume of 120 m^3 and base area of 30 m^2? ______________

Michael bought some cereal at the grocery store.

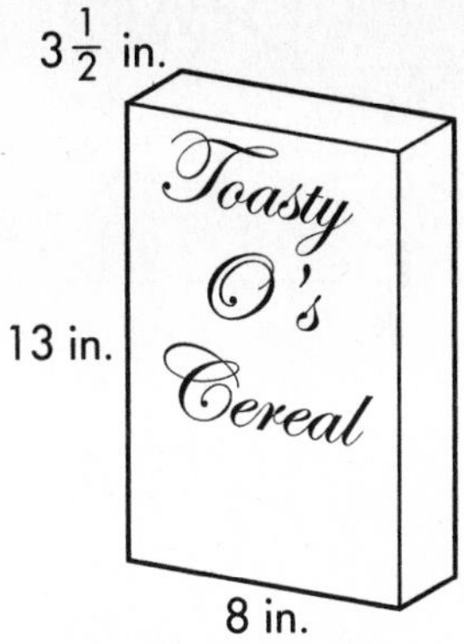

7. What is the base area of the box?

____

8. What is the volume of the box?

____

9. What is the base area of this figure?

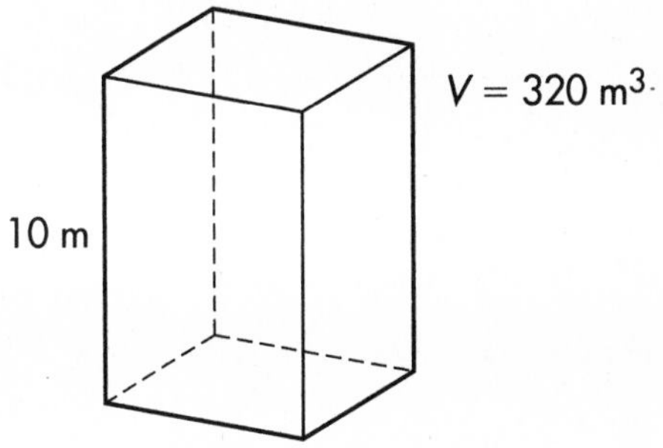

A 3.2 m^2 **C** 320 m^2

B 32 m^2 **D** 3,200 m^2

10. Explain It Explain how you would find the base area of a rectangular prism if you know the volume and the height.

____

Name ______________________

Practice
13-6

Irregular Shapes and Solids

For **1** and **2**, find the area of the irregular shape.

1.

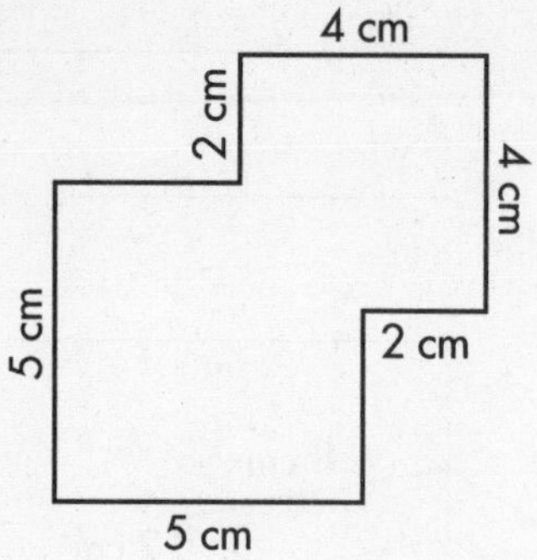

____

2.

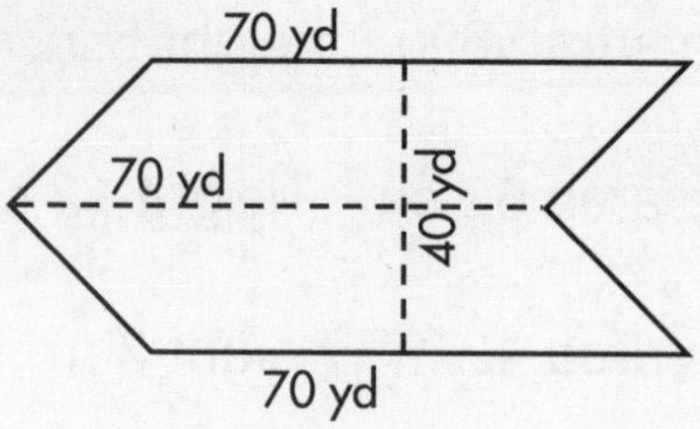

____

For **3** and **4**, find the volume of the irregular solid.

3.

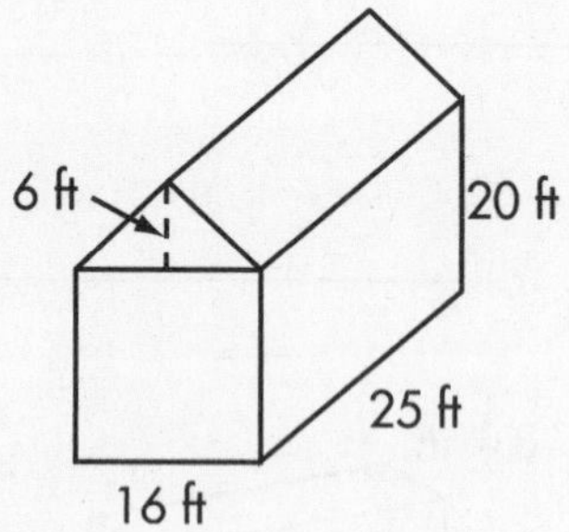

____

4.

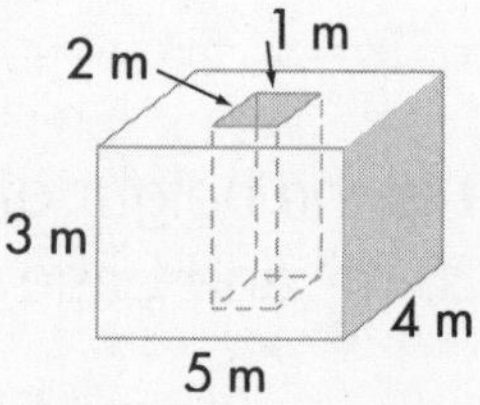

____

5. What is the area of this irregular shape?

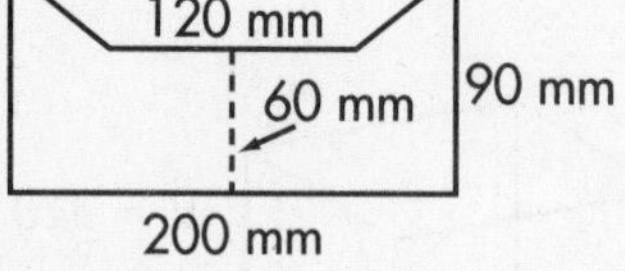

A 1,200 mm^2

B 12,000 mm^2

C 13,200 mm^2

D 14,400 mm^2

6. **Explain It** When do you find an area or volume by separating the figure into smaller figures?

____

____

Name ____________________

Practice 13-7

Problem Solving: Use Objects and Solve a Simpler Problem

Use objects to help you solve a simpler problem. Use the solution to help you solve the original problem.

1. **Number Sense** Six people can be seated at a table. If two tables are put together, 10 people can be seated. How many tables are needed to make a long table that will seat 22 people?

   ____

2. Donna is building a large cube that will have 5 layers, each with 5 rows of 5 small cubes. How many small cubes will the larger cube contain?

   ____

3. **Strategy Practice** Jerome's job duties include feeding the fish. There are 5 kinds of fish that he feeds: guppies, zebra danios, betas, platys, and neon tetras.
   Use the following clues to find the order in which Jerome feeds them.

   - Jerome feeds the guppies third.
   - Jerome does not feed the betas right before or right after the guppies.
   - Jerome feeds the zebra danios last.
   - Jerome feeds the platys after the betas.

   A guppies, zebra danios, betas, platys, and neon tetras
   B betas, platys, guppies, neon tetras, zebra danios
   C neon tetras, zebra danios, guppies, platys, betas
   D betas, guppies, platys, neon tetras, zebra danios

4. **Explain It** Suppose Ann is placing bowling pins in the following manner: 1 pin in the first row, 2 pins in the second row, 3 pins in the third row, and so on. How many pins will she use if she has 5 rows in her placement? Explain.

   ____

Name ______________________

Practice 14-1

Customary Units of Capacity

Which unit(s) of capacity would be most reasonable to measure each?

1. barrel of oil ______________

2. can of applesauce ______________

3. individual carton of orange juice ______________

Give the amount of liquid in each container. Use a fraction if necessary.

4. 

= ________ pt

5. 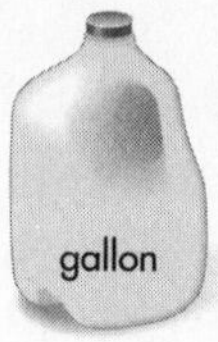

= ________ qt

6. **Reasoning** Do 1 gallon and 8 pints represent the same amount?

   A No, 8 pints is 8 times the amount of 1 gallon.

   B No, 1 gallon is equal to 4 quarts.

   C Yes, 1 gallon is equal to 4 quarts, which is equal to 8 pints.

   D Yes, 8 pints is equal to 8 cups, which is equal to 1 gallon.

7. **Explain It** If you only needed 1 c of milk, what is your best choice at the grocery store—a quart container, a pint container, or a $\frac{1}{2}$ gal container? Explain.

____

____

Name ______________________

Practice
14-2

Metric Units of Capacity

Estimation Which unit of capacity would be most reasonable to measure each?

1. bottle of water: 1 mL or 1 L ____________

2. bottle cap: 20 mL or 20 L ____________

3. swimming pool: 80,000 mL or 80,000 L ____________

Give the amount of liquid in each container.

4.

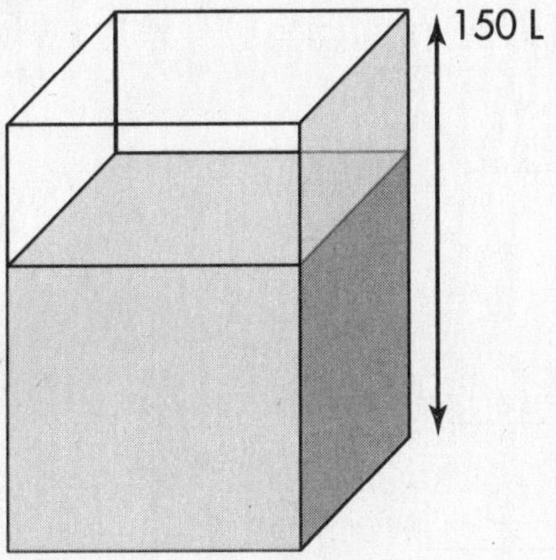

____

5.

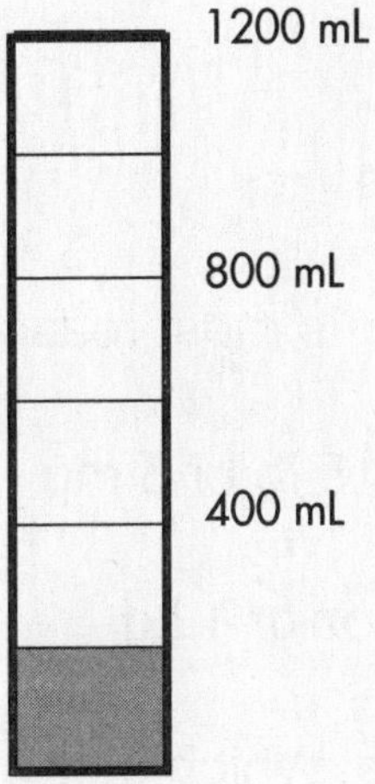

____

6. Reasonableness In a science fair project, you test four different-sized containers of water: 1 L, 2 L, 4 L, and 5 L. Which of the following expresses these capacities in milliliters?

A 1 mL, 2 mL, 4 mL, 5 mL
B 10 mL, 20 mL, 40 mL, 50 mL
C 100 mL, 200 mL, 400 mL, 500 mL
D 1,000 mL, 2,000 mL, 4,000 mL, 5,000 mL

7. Explain It Tell whether you would use multiplication or division to convert milliliters to liters. Explain your answer.

____

____

Name ______________________

Practice 14-3

Units of Weight and Mass

Which customary unit of weight would be best to measure each weight?

1. newborn baby ______________

2. earrings ______________

Which metric unit of mass would be better to measure each mass?

3. necktie ______________

4. 5 math textbooks ______________

Which mass or weight is most reasonable for each?

5. laptop computer: 5 lb or 5 mg ______________

6. dozen donuts: 1 oz or 1 kg ______________

7. **Reasonableness** Which unit would you use to weigh a garbage truck?

   A ton **B** kilogram **C** pound **D** milligram

8. **Explain It** Did you know that there is litter in outer space? Humans exploring space have left behind bags of trash, bolts, gloves, and pieces of satellites. Suppose there are about 4,000,000 lb of litter in orbit around Earth. About how many tons of space litter is this? Explain how you found your answer.

   ____

Name ______________________________

Converting Customary Units

In **1** through **9**, convert each measurement. You may need to convert more than once.

1. 3,520 yd = _____ mi
2. 10 ft 5 in. = _____ in.
3. 3 T = __________ oz

4. 4 gal = _____ c
5. 2 gal = _____ fl oz
6. 6 yd 2 ft = _____ in.

7. 6 qt 1 pt = _____ pt
8. 40 qt = _____ gal
9. 48 ft = _____ yd

10. Jenny bought a gallon of orange juice. The recipe for punch calls for 2 quarts of juice. How many quarts will she have left over to drink at breakfast?

____

11. Algebra Laura has a roll of ribbon. There are 20 yards of ribbon on the roll. What equation can Laura use to find the number of inches of ribbon on the roll?

____

12. Ramona drives a truck weighing 1 ton. She picks up 3 cows weighing 3,000 pounds total. How much do the truck and the cows weigh together?

A 50 lb
B 500 lb
C 5,000 lb
D 50,000 lb

13. Explain It If you want to convert pounds to ounces, do you multiply or divide?

____

____

Name ______________________

Practice **14-5**

Converting Metric Units

In **1** through **6**, convert each measurement.

1. 3,000 mm = ________ m

2. 8 km = ________ m

3. 6 m = ________ cm

4. 9.8 kg = ________ g

5. 20,000 mg = ________ g

6. 11,000 mL = ________ L

In **7** through **12**, compare the measurements.
Use <, >, or = for each ◯.

7. 4,000 g ◯ 5 kg

8. 0.72 L ◯ 572 mL

9. 5.12 m ◯ 512 cm

10. 8 kg ◯ 5,000 g

11. 44 L ◯ 44,000 mL

12. 200 m ◯ 20,000 mm

13. A watering can holds 4.2 liters. If a small cactus requires 310 mL of water once every 3 weeks, how many of the same cactus plant can be watered at once without refilling the watering can?

____

14. Critical Thinking How do you convert kilometers to meters?

____

15. Jeremy's apartment building is 15 meters tall. How many centimeters is this?

A 1.5 cm **B** 50 cm **C** 1,500 cm **D** 15,000 cm

16. Explain It Explain how to convert 24 kilograms to grams.

____

____

____

Name ______________________

Practice
14-6

Elapsed Time

Find each elapsed time.

1. 9:59 P.M. to 10:45 P.M. ______________

2. 1:45 P.M. to 5:38 P.M. ______________

3.

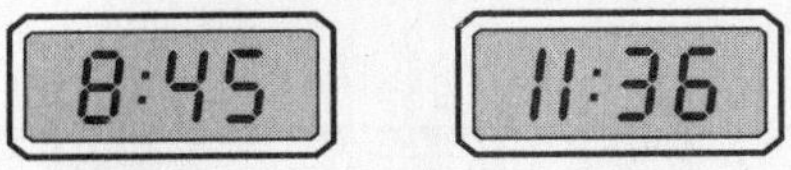

A.M. A.M.

____

4.

P.M. P.M.

____

Find the end time using the given elapsed time.

5. Start: 3:46 P.M. Elapsed: 2 h 20 min ______________

6. Add. 2 h 45 min
+ 3 h 58 min

7. Add. 6 h 47 min
+ 5 h 28 min

The White House Visitor Center is open from 7:30 A.M. until 4:00 P.M.

8. Tara and Miguel got to the Visitor Center when it opened, and spent 1 hour and 20 minutes there. At what time did they leave? ______________

9. Jennifer left the Visitor Center at 3:30 P.M. after spending 40 minutes there. At what time did she arrive? ______________

10. A football game lasted 2 hours and 37 minutes. It finished at 4:22 P.M. When did it start?

A 1:45 p.m **B** 1:55 p.m **C** 2:45 p.m **D** 2:50 p.m

11. **Explain It** What is 1 hour and 35 minutes before 4:05 p.m? Explain how you solved this problem.

____

Name ______________________________

Practice
14-7

Elapsed Time in Other Units

Find the elapsed time.

1. 9:50 P.M. to 4:00 A.M. ______________

2. 5:15 A.M. to 2:15 P.M. ______________

3. 10:00 P.M. to 4:45 A.M. ______________

4. 6:30 P.M. to 5:10 A.M. ______________

Find the end or start time.

5. Start time: 8:15 A.M.
   Elapsed time: 30 h 20 min.

   ____

6. End time: 10:30 P.M.
   Elapsed time: 13 h 30 min.

   ____

7. **Number Sense** Krishan wakes up at 7:30 A.M. every morning. He spends 30 minutes getting ready, 6 hours at school, and 2 hours volunteering. Then he takes the bus for 15 minutes and arrives at his house. What time does he arrive at his house?

   A 2:00 P.M. **B** 3:45 P.M. **C** 4:15 P.M. **D** 5:45 P.M.

8. **Explain It** Emre left for a trip Sunday night at 10:00 P.M. He returned home Tuesday morning at 6:00 A.M. How many hours was he away on his trip? Explain how you found your answer.

   ____

   ____

   ____

Name ______________________________

Temperature Change

Write each temperature in Celsius and Fahrenheit.

1. 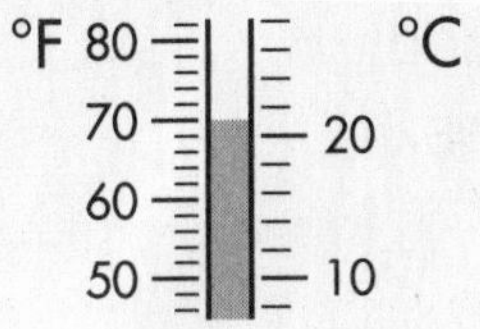

______, ______

2. 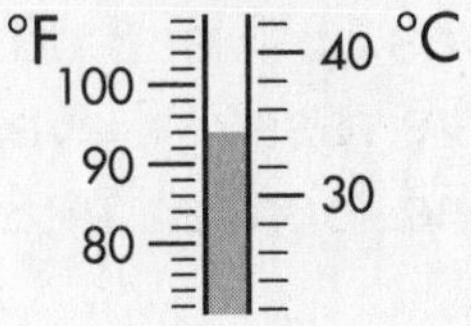

______, ______

3. 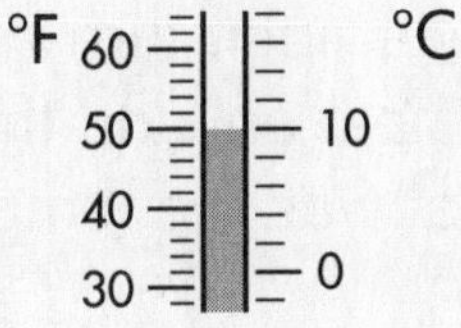

______, ______

Find each change in temperature.

4. 34°F to 67°F

____

5. 12°C to 7°C

____

6. Number Sense Which is a smaller increase in temperature: a 5°F increase or a 5°C increase?

____

Information about the record high temperatures in four states is shown.

Record High Temperature

State	°F	°C
Alaska	100	38
Florida	109	43
Michigan	112	44
Hawaii	100	38

7. What is the difference between the record high temperature in Florida and the record high temperature in Alaska in °C?

____

8. What is the difference between the record high temperature in Michigan and the record high temperature in Florida in °F? ______

9. What is the difference between −6°C and 12°C?

A 6°C **B** 12°C **C** 18°C **D** 19°C

10. Explain It Which is warmer, 1°F or 1°C? Explain how you found this answer.

____

____

Name ________________________________

Problem Solving: Make a Table

Make a table to solve the problems.

1. The temperature in the room was 55°F at 8:00 A.M. Ed turned the heat on, and the temperature rose 4°F every 30 minutes. What was the temperature of the room at 11:30 A.M.?

____

2. Charles can type 72 words per minute. He needs to type a paper with 432 words. How many minutes will it take Charles to type the paper?

____

3. **Number Sense** Yugita wakes up at 5:00 A.M. on Monday. Each day after that, she wakes up 17 minutes later. What time will she wake up on Friday?

   A 5:17 A.M.

   B 5:51 A.M.

   C 6:08 A.M.

   D 6:25 A.M.

4. **Explain It** Train A leaves from New York at 10:15 A.M. and arrives in New Haven at 12:23 P.M. Train B takes 2 hours to go from New York to New Haven, but takes a 20-minute rest break in the middle of the trip. Which train is faster? Explain.

____

____

Name ______________________

Solving Addition and Subtraction Equations

Solve and check each equation.

1. $x + 4 = 16$ ______________
2. $t - 8 = 15$ ______________
3. $m - 9 = 81$ ______________
4. $7 + y = 19$ ______________
5. $k - 10 = 25$ ______________
6. $15 + b = 50$ ______________
7. $f + 18 = 20$ ______________
8. $w - 99 = 100$ ______________
9. $75 + n = 100$ ______________
10. $p - 40 = 0$ ______________

11. Jennifer has $14. She sold a notebook and pen, and now she has $18. Solve the equation $14 + m = 18$ to find how much money Jennifer received by selling the notebook and pen.

____

12. Kit Carson was born in 1809. He died in 1868. Use the equation $1{,}809 + x = 1{,}868$ to find how many years Kit Carson lived.

____

13. **Strategy Practice** Which is the solution for y when $y - 6 = 19$?

A 13 **B** 15 **C** 23 **D** 25

14. **Explain It** Nellie solved $y - 3 = 16$. Is her answer correct? Explain and find the correct answer if she is incorrect.

$y - 3 = 16$
$y = 13$
Subtract 3

____

____

____

____

____

Name ___________________________

Practice
15-2

Solving Multiplication and Division Equations

Solve each equation.

1. $11y = 55$ __________

2. $\frac{c}{9} = 6$ __________

3. $150 = 25p$ __________

4. $16 = \frac{w}{4}$ __________

5. $\frac{k}{36} = 8$ __________

6. $13d = 39$ __________

7. $30 = 10x$ __________

8. $\frac{m}{7} = 13$ __________

9. $81 = 9t$ __________

10. $5b = 30$ __________

11. $20 = 4a$ __________

12. $\frac{e}{80} = 2$ __________

13. Reasoning Antoinette divides 54 by 9 to solve an equation for y. One side of the equation is 54. Write the equation.

____

14. Adam is making a trout dinner for six people. He buys 48 oz of trout. How many ounces of trout will each person get?

____

15. Which operation would you use to solve the equation $19x = 646$?

A add 19 **B** subtract 17 **C** divide by 19 **D** multiply by 19

16. Explain It How would you use mental math to find m in the equation $63\left(\frac{m}{63}\right) = 2$?

____

____

Name ____________________

Practice
15-3

Inequalities and the Number Line

Name three solutions of each inequality. Then graph each inequality on a number line.

1. $b \geq 5$

____

2. $s + 2 \leq 4$

____

3. $x \leq 3$

____

4. $d - 1 \geq 6$

____

5. Lizette wants to read more books. Her goal is to read at least 2 books each month. Let *m* represent the number of books she will read in a year. Use $m \geq 24$ to graph the number of books she plans to read on a number line.

6. Estimation Marcus is making cookies for his class. There are 26 students, and he wants to bring 3 cookies per student. On Sunday, he runs out of time and decides he must buy at least half the cookies and will make no more than half from scratch. Draw a graph to represent how many cookies he will make himself.

7. Which sentence is graphed on the line below?

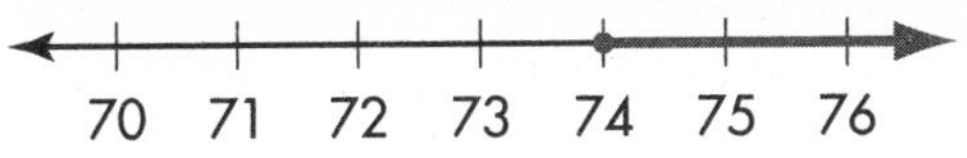

A $m > 74$ **B** $m \geq 74$ **C** $m = 74$ **D** $m < 74$

8. Explain It How do you know whether to use an open circle or a closed circle when graphing an inequality?

____

____

Name ______________________

Practice 15-4

Patterns and Equations

For **1** through **3**, find a rule for each table. Write an equation for each rule.

1.

x	y
5	15
2	6
11	33
6	18

______

2.

x	y
18	9
50	25
12	6
34	17

______

3.

x	y
4	–4
8	0
12	4
16	8

______

4. Reasoning Write an equation that will give the answer $y = 5$ when $x = 12$.

____

5. A farmer sells 200 apples at the market. The next week, he sells 345 apples. How many more apples did he sell the second week?

____

6. In the equation $y = x - 5$, which numbers would you use for x if you wanted $y < 0$?

A numbers < 10 **B** 1, 2, 3, 4 **C** 6, 7, 8 **D** 10, 11, 12

7. Explain It If you know the rule for a table, how can you add pairs of numbers to the table?

____

____

Name ______________________________

Practice
15-5

Problem Solving: Draw a Picture and Write an Equation

Draw a picture, write, and solve an equation to answer the question.

1. Suki and Amy made a total of 15 homemade holiday cards. Amy gave away 7 of them. How many cards did Suki give away?

2. Ramon ate 3 more pieces of fruit today than he did yesterday. Today he ate 4 pieces. Write an equation to find out how many pieces of fruit he ate yesterday.

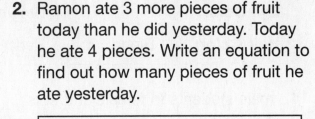

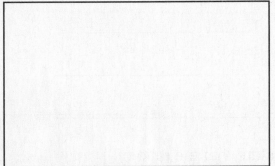

3. Critical Thinking A total of 64 children are going on a field trip. If 14 of the children are girls, how many are boys?

____

____

4. Naomi's class went to the museum. There are 16 students in her class. If the total cost of admission for the class was $96, what does one admission to the museum cost?

____

____

5. Paul is in a 17-kilometer canoe race. He has just reached the 5-kilometer marker. Which of the following equations can you use to find out how many more kilometers he needs to paddle?

A $k - 5 = 17$ **B** $5 + k = 17$ **C** $5 - k = 17$ **D** $17 + 5 = k$

6. Explain It How can you use estimation to decide whether 24.50 multiplied by 4 is close to 100?

____

Name ______________________________

Understanding Ratios

Use the chart below in **1** through **4** to write each ratio three ways.

Mr. White's 3rd-Grade Class (24 Students)

Gender:	Male	8	Female	16				
Eye Color:	Blue	6	Brown	4	Hazel	12	Green	2
Hair Color:	Blond	5	Red	1	Brown	15	Black	3

1. male students to female students ______________

2. female students to male students ______________

3. red-haired students to all students ______________

4. all students to green-eyed students ______________

5. Reasonableness Is it reasonable to state that the ratio of male students to female students is the same as the ratio of male students to all students? Explain.

____

____

6. George has 2 sons and 1 daughter. What is the ratio of daughters to sons?

A 2 to 1 **B** 1 to 2 **C** 3:1 **D** $\frac{2}{1}$

7. Explain It The ratio of blue beads to white beads in a necklace is 3:8. Nancy says that for every 11 beads, 3 are blue. Do you agree? Explain.

____

____

____

Name ______________________

Practice 16-2

Understanding Percent

Write the fraction in lowest terms and the percent that represents the shaded part of each figure.

1. 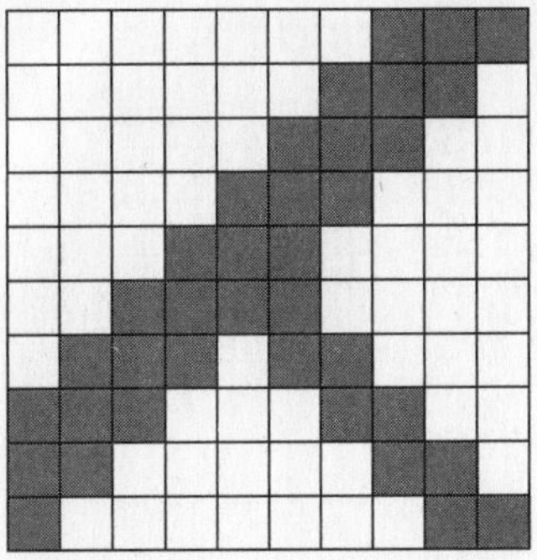

____

2. 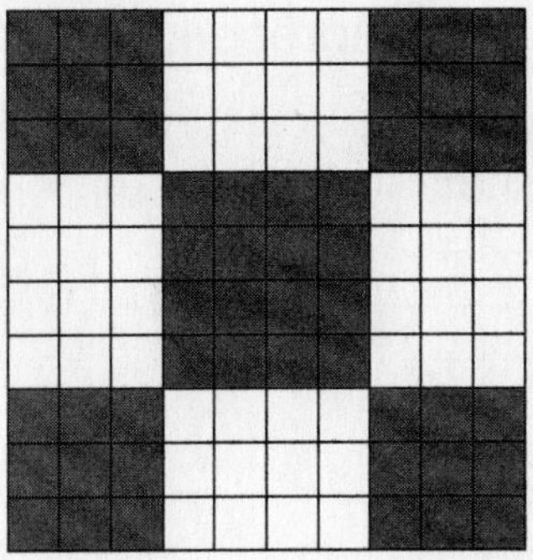

____

3. Strategy Practice In the square, if part A is $\frac{1}{4}$ of the square and part C is $\frac{1}{10}$ of the square, what percent of the square is part B?

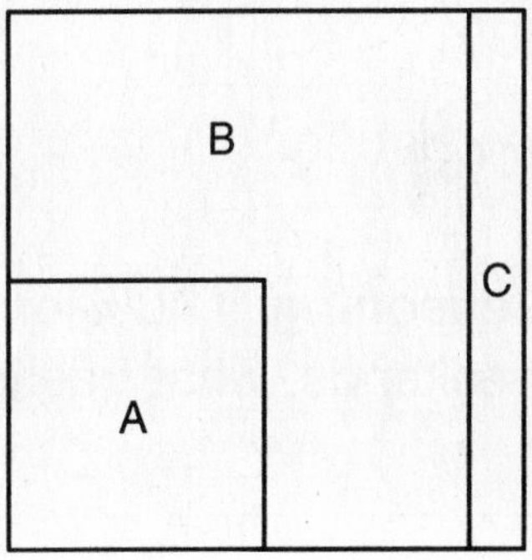

____

4. In Russia, $\frac{1}{4}$ of the land is covered by forests. What percent of Russia is covered by forest? What percent of Russia is not covered by forest?

____

5. In the United States, $\frac{3}{10}$ of the land is forests and woodland. What percent of the United States is forest and woodland?

____

6. If $\frac{2}{5}$ of a figure is shaded, what percent is not shaded?

A 20% **B** 30% **C** 50% **D** 60%

7. Explain It Explain how a decimal is related to a percent.

____

____

Name ________________________

Percents, Fractions, and Decimals

For questions **1** through **3**, write the percent, decimal, and fraction in simplest form represented by the shaded part of each 100-grid.

1. 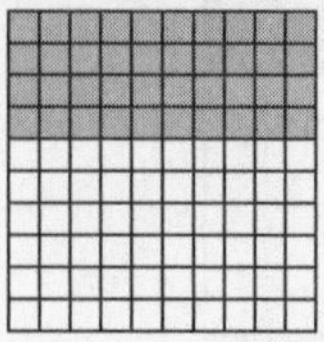
____

2. 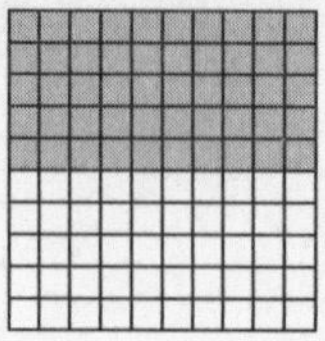
____

3. 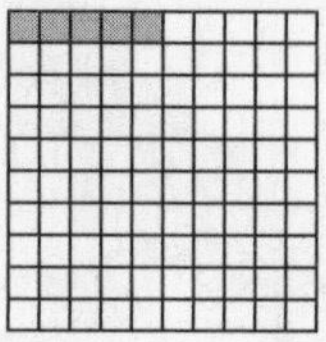
____

For questions **4** through **9**, write each percent as a decimal and a fraction in simplest form.

4. 30% ________ **5.** 60% ________ **6.** 32% ________

7. 11% ________ **8.** 150% ________ **9.** 100% ________

10. Reasoning If 40% of Jeanne's friends play kickball on weekends, what fraction of her friends don't play kickball?

____

11. If there are 6 eggs in 50% of an egg crate, how many eggs are in the whole crate?

____

12. What would you do first to order the following numbers from least to greatest?

30%, $\frac{2}{3}$, 0.67, $\frac{8}{9}$, 0.7

A Order the decimals.

B Convert the decimals to percents.

C Order the fractions.

D Convert all numbers to decimals.

13. Explain It When writing a percent as a decimal, why do you move the decimal point 2 places?

____

Name ______________________

Finding Percent of a Whole Number

Find each using mental math.

1. 20% of 60 ______
2. 30% of 500 ______
3. 25% of 88 ______
4. 70% of 30 ______
5. **Reasoning** Order these numbers from least to greatest.
   0.85, $\frac{1}{4}$, 72%, $\frac{5}{8}$, 20%, 0.3

   ____

6. What is 40% of 240?

   A 48 **B** 96 **C** 128 **D** 960

The table below shows the percent of the population that live in rural and urban areas of each country. Use the table to answer **7** through **9**.

	Rural	Urban
Bermuda	0%	100%
Cuba	25%	75%
Guatemala	60%	40%

7. Out of every 300 people in Cuba, how many of them live in a rural area? ______________________
8. Out of every 1,000 people in Guatemala, how many live in urban areas? ______________________
9. **Explain It** If there are 1,241,356 people who live in Bermuda, how many residents of Bermuda live in urban areas? How many live in rural areas? Explain your answer.

   ____

   ____

Name ______________________

Practice
16-5

Problem Solving: Make a Table and Look for a Pattern

For exercises **1** through **4**, find each percent by completing each table.

1. 12 out of 40 days were rainy. __________

Rainy days	12			
Total days	40	20	10	

2. 2 out of 8 marbles are blue. __________

Blue	2			
Total marbles	8	16	4	

3. 32 out of 40 days were windy. __________

Windy days	32			
Total days	40	5	20	

4. 16 out of 40 pets on Jack's street are dogs. __________

Dogs	16			
Total pets	40	80	10	

5. Write a Problem Write a real-world problem that you can solve using a table to find a percent.

____

____

6. Emmy plans to hike 32 miles this weekend. On Saturday, she hiked 24 miles. What percent of her goal has Emmy hiked?

____

7. Explain It Dave estimated 45% of 87 by finding 50% of 90. Will his estimate be greater than or less than the exact answer?

____

Name ________________________________

Understanding Integers

Write an integer for each word description.

1. a withdrawal of $50 **2.** a temperature rise of 14° **3.** 10° below zero

__________ __________ __________

Use the number line for **4** through **7.** Write the integer for each point.

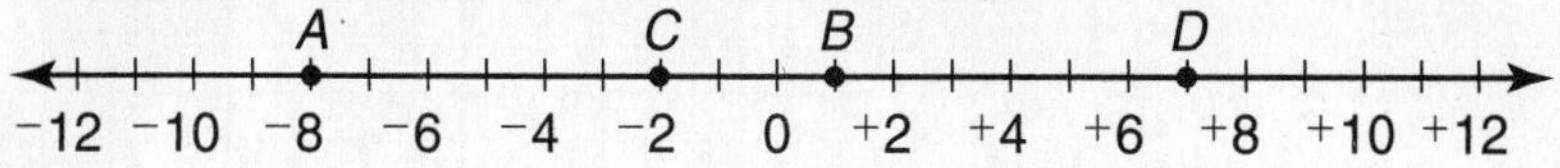

4. *A* ________ **5.** *B* ________ **6.** *C* ________ **7.** *D* ________

Compare. Use >, <, or = for each ◯.

8. −5 ◯ −9 **9.** $^+8$ ◯ −12 **10.** $^+21$ ◯ −26

Write in order from least to greatest.

11. $^-4$, $^+11$, $^-11$, $^+4$ ________, ________, ________, ________

12. $^-6$, $^+6$, 0, $^-14$ ________, ________, ________, ________

13. $^+11$, $^-8$, $^+7$, $^-4$ ________, ________, ________, ________

14. **Strategy Practice** Which point is farthest to the right on a number line?

A −6 **B** −2 **C** 0 **D** 2

15. **Explain It** In Fenland, U.K., the elevation from sea level is $^-4$*m.* In San Diego, U.S., it is $^+40$ ft. The elevations are given in different units. Explain how to tell which location has a greater elevation.

____

____

____

Name ______________________

Practice **17-2**

Ordered Pairs

Write the ordered pair for each point.

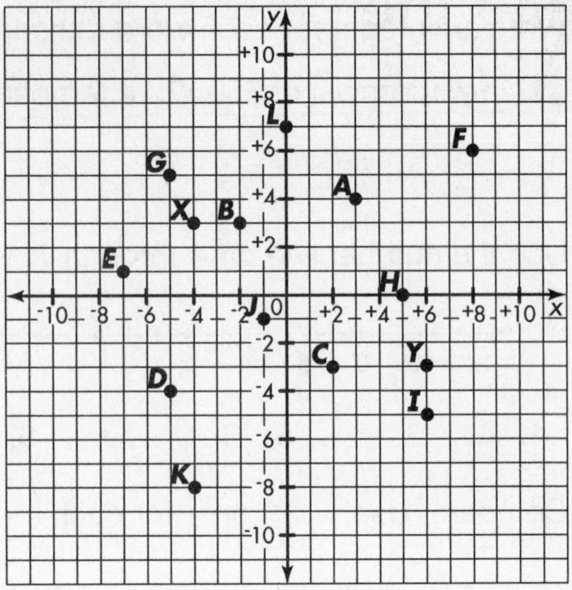

1. *A* ________
2. *B* ________
3. *C* ________
4. *D* ________
5. *E* ________
6. *F* ________

Name the point for each ordered pair.

7. (+5, 0) ________
8. (−1, −1) ________
9. (0, +7) ________
10. (+6, −5) ________
11. (−4, −8) ________
12. (−5, +5) ________

13. **Strategy Practice** If a taxicab were to start at the point (0, 0) and drive 6 units left, 3 units down, 1 unit right, and 9 units up, what ordered pair would name the point the cab would finish at? ________

14. Use the coordinate graph above. Which is the *y*-coordinate for point *X*?

A +6 **B** +3 **C** −3 **D** −6

15. **Explain It** Explain how to graph the ordered pair (−2, +3).

____

____

____

____

Name ______________________

Distances on Number Lines and the Coordinate Plane

Find the distance between each pair of integers on a number line.

1. −7, −3 ________

2. −7, 1 ________

3. −4, 0 ________

4. 0, 5 ________

5. 2, 8 ________

6. −3, 3 ________

Find the distance between the points named by each set of ordered pairs on the coordinate plane.

7. (−2, 5), (−2, −1) ________

8. (−4, 1), (0, 1) ________

9. (−1, 7), (−1, −2) ________

10. (−2, −6), (−1, −6) ________

11. At 2:00 P.M., the temperature was 3°C. By 4:00 P.M., the temperature had dropped to −1°C. What was the amount of the decrease in temperature?

____

12. **Strategy Practice** What integer on a number line is the same distance from 0 as $^{+}4$?

____

13. On the coordinate plane, what is the distance between the points named by ($^{+}2$, $^{-}6$) and ($^{-}3$, $^{-}4$), if you move only along the lines of the grid?

A 11 **B** 9 **C** 7 **D** −7

14. **Explain It** How can you tell if two points lie along the same grid line just by looking at the ordered pairs?

____

____

____

Name ____________________

Practice 17-4

Graphing Equations

In **1** through **4**, find the value of y when $x = 4$, 9, and 15.

1. $y = 2x$ ____________ **2.** $y = x - 4$ ____________

3. $y = 4x$ ____________ **4.** $y = x + 6$ ____________

In **5** through **8**, make a table of values for each equation and then graph the equations. Let $x = 1$, 3, 5, and 7.

5. $y = x + 2$ ____________ **6.** $y = 3x$ ____________

7. $y = x - 1$ ____________ **8.** $y = x + 5$ ____________

9. Reasoning Without drawing the graph, describe what the graph of $x = 100$ would look like. Explain.

____

____

____

10. Reasonableness Which of the following ordered pairs is **NOT** on the graph of the equation $y = x + 9$?

A (7, 16) **B** (15, 24) **C** (20, 29) **D** (28, 36)

11. Explain It A graph contains the ordered pair (2, 4). Write two different equations that would be possible for this graph. Explain how you found your answer.

____

____

____

Name ______________________

Problem Solving: Work Backward

Solve each problem by working backward. Write the answers in complete sentences.

Barbara is refilling her bird feeders and squirrel feeders in her yard.

1. After filling her bird feeders, Barbara has $3\frac{1}{2}$ c of mixed birdseed left. The two feeders in the front yard took $4\frac{1}{2}$ c each. The two feeders in the backyard each took $2\frac{3}{4}$ c. The two feeders next to the living room window each took $3\frac{1}{4}$ c. How much mixed birdseed did Barbara have before filling the feeders?

   ____

2. After Barbara fills each of her 4 squirrel feeders with $2\frac{2}{3}$ c of peanuts, she has $1\frac{3}{4}$ c of peanuts left. How many cups of peanuts did Barbara start with?

   ____

3. **Strategy Practice** Clint spends $\frac{1}{4}$ hour practicing trumpet, $\frac{1}{2}$ hour doing tasks around the house, $1\frac{1}{2}$ hour doing homework, and $\frac{3}{4}$ hour cleaning his room. He is finished at 7:30 P.M. When did Clint start?

   A 4:00 P.M. **B** 4:15 P.M. **C** 4:30 P.M. **D** 5:30 P.M.

4. **Write a Problem** Write a real-world problem that you can solve by working backward.

   ____

   ____

Name ______________________________

Practice
18-1

Data from Surveys

Ms. Chen's class took a survey on how many minutes it took each student to get to school. The results are below:

12   14   5   22   18   12   12   6   14   18   12   5   11

1. What are the highest and lowest times? ____________

2. Make a line plot to display the data.

Students in Ms. Chen's Class

Music Bought in Class B

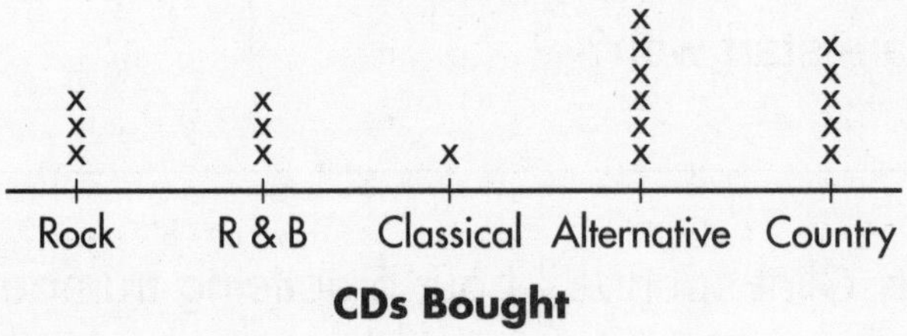

3. If the entire class responded to the survey, how many students are in the class? ____________

4. What information was collected about music?

____

5. Use the line plot above. Which type of CDs did students buy most often?

A Alternative   **B** Classical   **C** Country   **D** Rock

6. **Explain It** Write a survey question that might gather the following information. "In one school there are 6 sets of twins, 2 sets of triplets, and one set of quadruplets."

____

____

Name ______________________________

Bar Graphs and Picture Graphs

In **1** and **2**, answer the questions about the double-bar graph below.

1. How many boys play indoor soccer? How many girls play?

____

____

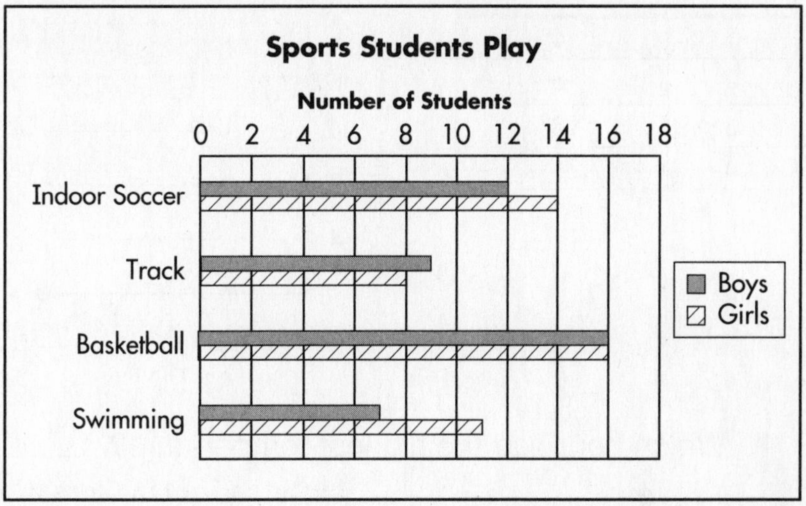

2. What is the least popular sport among girls? Among boys?

____

____

____

3. Frank bought 4 dozen doughnuts for his class. He had 4 left over. Which shows how to find how many doughnuts Frank gave away?

A $(48 \times 2) - 4$
B $(24 \times 2) - 12$
C $(12 \times 2) + 4$
D $(12 \times 4) - 4$

4. Explain It Could the data in the bar graph in Exercise 1 be presented in a picture graph? Explain.

____

____

____

____

Name ______________________

Practice
18-3

Line Graphs

Display the data in the table below on a coordinate grid.

Hour	Temperature (Celsius)
1	4°
2	8°
3	16°
4	21°

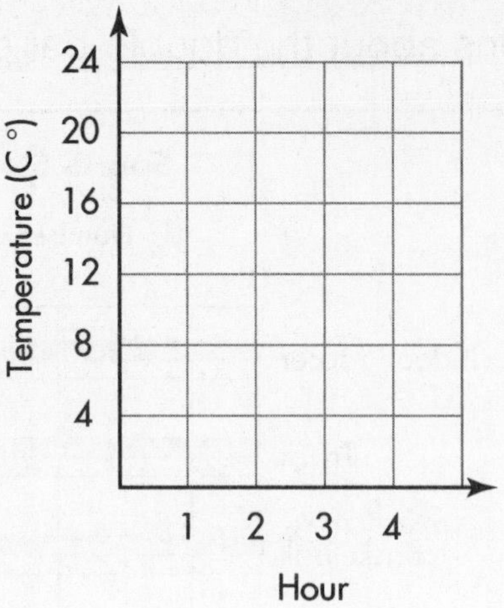

1. Which hour had the highest temperature? ______________

2. How much higher was the temperature in Hour 4 than Hour 1? ______________

3. Reasoning If Hour 1 was really 10:00 P.M., do you think the trend on the line graph would keep increasing? Explain.

____

____

4. Critical Thinking Look at the line graph at the right. What do you know about the trend of the housing prices?

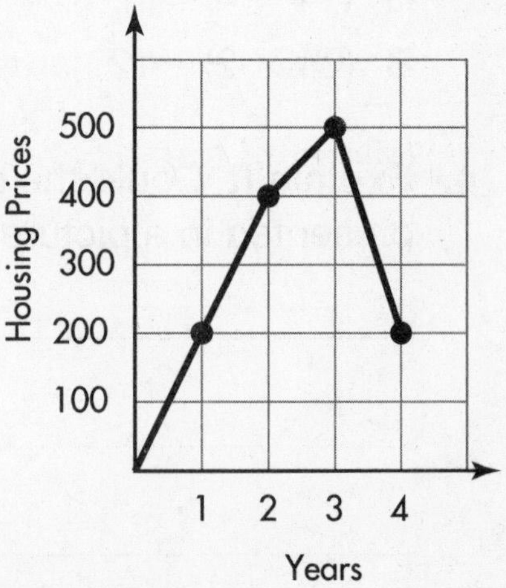

A Housing prices increased.

B Housing prices decreased.

C Housing prices increased, then decreased.

D Housing prices decreased, then increased.

5. Explain It In the example above, if housing prices had stayed the same for all four years, what would the line graph look like? Explain.

____

____

Name ______________________________

Practice
18-4

Stem-and-Leaf Plots

For **1** through **3**, use the stem-and-leaf plot below. It shows the ages of the 17 people who used the outdoor pool from 6:00 A.M. to 7:00 A.M. on a Tuesday morning in the summer.

Ages (years)

Stem	**Leaf**
0	
1	1
2	3 9
3	
4	7
5	5 7 7 9
6	5 5 6 6 7 8 9
7	0 1

Key: 7 | 1 means 71

1. How many swimmers were younger than 30?

____

2. Which age group was swimming the most at this hour?

____

____

3. Why are there two 5's as leaves next to the stem 6?

____

____

4. Make a stem-and-leaf plot of the data below.

Prices of couch pillows (dollars)			
10	75	20	20
37	24	21	9

5. Refer to the stem-and-leaf plot in Exercise 4. Which stem (or stems) have the most leaves?

A 70 **B** 9 **C** 20 **D** 30

Name ____________________

Practice
18-5

Histograms

This table shows the results of a class survey to find out how many pieces of fruit each student ate that week.

Amount of Fruit	Frequency
0–7	12
8–15	8
16–25	5

1. Complete the histogram below. What percentage of students ate 16–25 pieces of fruit that week?

____

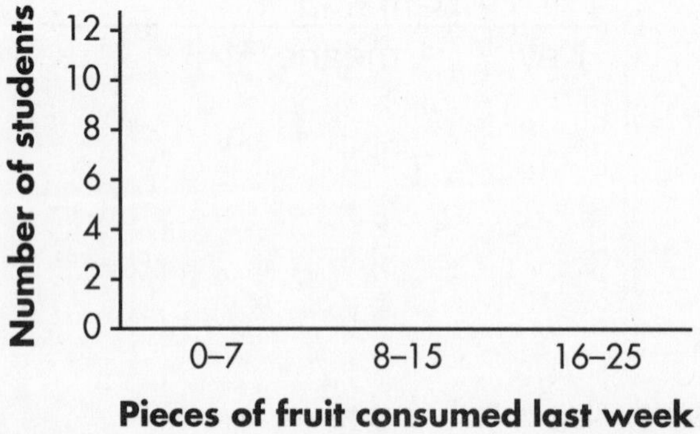

2. Reasoning Mary says a histogram shows that about 3 times as many people in the 60–79 age group answered a survey as in the 80–99 age group. How does she know this from looking at the histogram?

____

____

3. Explain It A political campaign recorded the ages of 100 callers. In a histogram, which data would go on the horizontal axis and which on the vertical?

____

____

Name ______________________________

Circle Graphs

1. A bagel shop offers a variety of bagels. One morning, the following choices were made by the first 20 customers of the day: plain, 10; poppy seed, 5; sesame seed, 3; multigrain, 2. Complete the table below.

	Fraction	Percent
Plain		
Poppy Seed		
Sesame Seed		
Multigrain		

2. Copy and complete the circle graph below with the data in the table above. Label each section with the percent and fraction of each bagel.

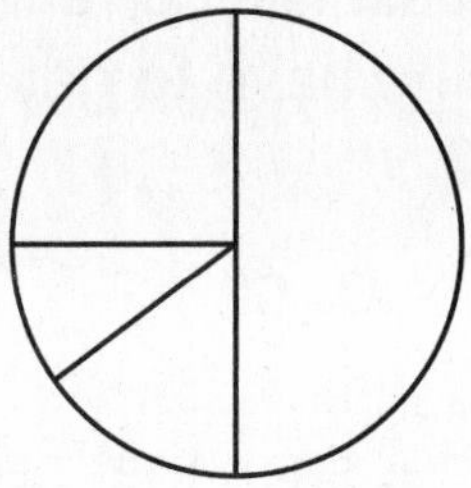

3. **Number Sense** A circle graph is divided into four sections. One section equals 40%. The other three sections are equal in size. What percent does each of the other three sections represent?

____

4. **Reasoning** If 10 out of 30 students in a survey chose ice skating as their favorite sport, what fraction of the circle should be shaded to represent the students who chose ice skating? How many degrees will that segment of the circle include?

____

Name ______________________

Practice
18-7

Mean

Find the mean of each set of data.

1. 2, 5, 9, 4 ____________

2. 44, 73, 63 ____________

3. 11, 38, 65, 4, 67 ____________

4. 3, 6, 3, 7, 8 ____________

5. 120, 450, 630 ____________

6. 4.2, 5.3, 7.1, 4.0, 11.9 ____________

Gene's bowling scores were as follows: 8, 4, 10, 10, 9, 6, 9.

7. What was his average bowling score? ____________

8. If Gene gets two more strikes (scores of 10), what is his new average? ____________

9. **Reasoning** Krishan wants his quiz average to be at least 90 so that he can get an A in the class. His current quiz scores are: 80, 100, 85. What does he have to get on his next quiz to have an average of 90?

A 85 **B** 90 **C** 92 **D** 95

10. **Explain It** Suppose Krishan's teacher says that he can drop one of his test scores. Using his test scores of 80, 100, and 85, which one should he drop, and why? What is his new average?

____

____

Name ______________________________

Practice
18-8

Median, Mode, and Range

1. Find the range of this data set: 225 342 288 552 263. ____________

2. Find the median of this data set: 476 234 355 765 470. ____________

3. Find the mode of this data set:
16 7 8 5 16 7 8 4 7 8 16 7. ____________

4. Find the range of this data set:
64 76 46 88 88 43 99 50 55. ____________

5. **Reasoning** Would the mode change if a 76 were added to the data in Exercise 4?

____

____

The table below gives the math test scores for Mrs. Jung's fifth-grade class.

76	54	92	88	76	88
75	93	92	68	88	76
76	88	80	70	88	72

Test Scores

6. Find the mean of the data. ____________

7. Find the mode of the data. ____________

8. Find the median of the data. ____________

9. What is the range of the data set? ____________

10. Find the range of this data set: 247, 366, 785, 998.

A 998 **B** 781 **C** 751 **D** 538

11. **Explain It** Will a set of data always have a mode? Explain your answer.

____

____

Name ______________________________

Practice
18-9

Problem Solving: Make a Graph

1. In a survey, 100 students from around the country were asked what news source they preferred. Which news source is most popular? Make a circle graph to solve the problem.

News Source	Number of Votes
Television	48
Internet	27
Newspaper	15
Radio	10

2. In a survey, 30 students from around the country were asked how they traveled to and from school. Make a circle graph to show the data.

Subway	Bus	Bike	On Foot	Taxi
6	12	4	8	0

3. If a graph shows that there were 10 people who watched between 7 and 12 movies, what kind of graph could you be looking at?

A Circle **B** Bar **C** Histogram **D** Line

4. **Explain It** Would a line graph be an appropriate graph in Exercise 3? Why or why not?

____

____

____

____

Name ______________________________

Translations

Give the vertical and horizontal translation in units.

1.

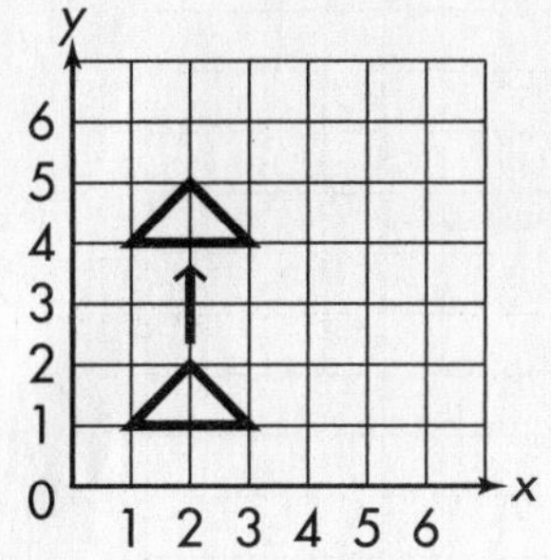

____

2.

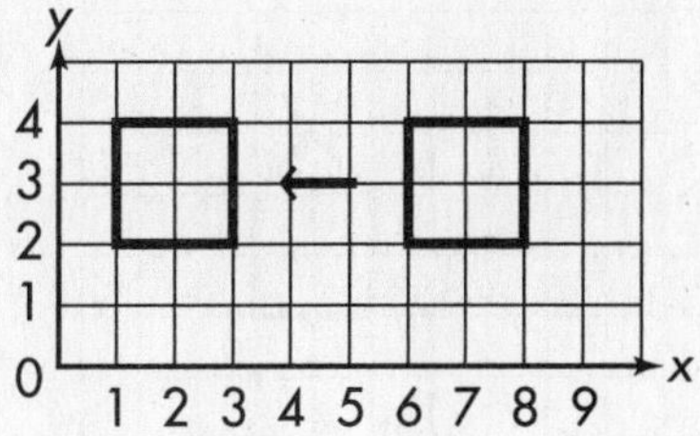

____

3.

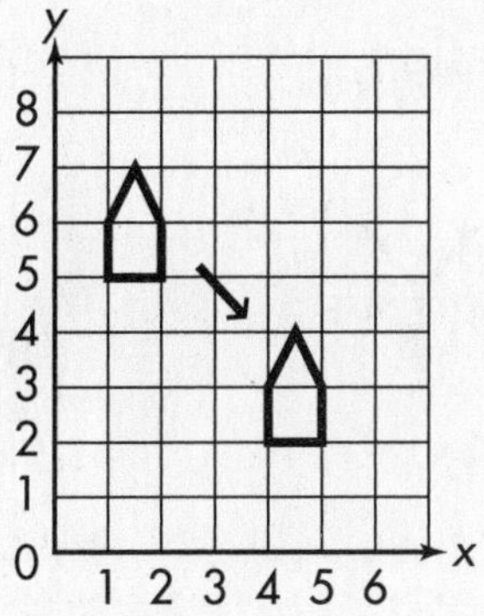

____

4.

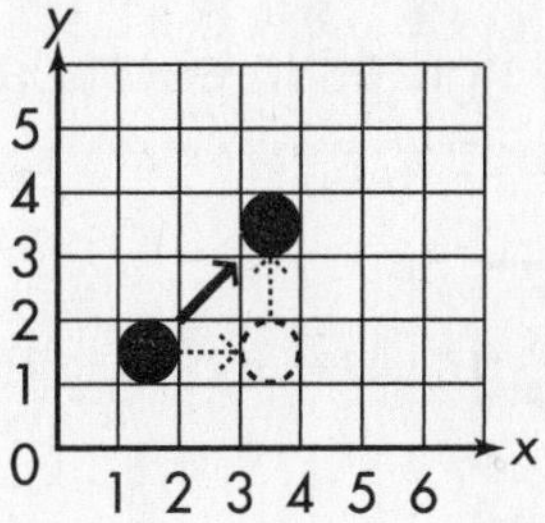

____

5. Critical Thinking If an object moves from the first quadrant into the third quadrant, which of the following is a possible move?

A 4 up, 2 right

B 5 down, 5 right

C 2 up, 8 left

D 6 down, 4 left

6. Explain It Explain how the *x* and *y* coordinates are related to the direction an object moves.

____

____

____

____

Name ____________________

Reflections

Draw the reflection of the object across the reflection line.

1.

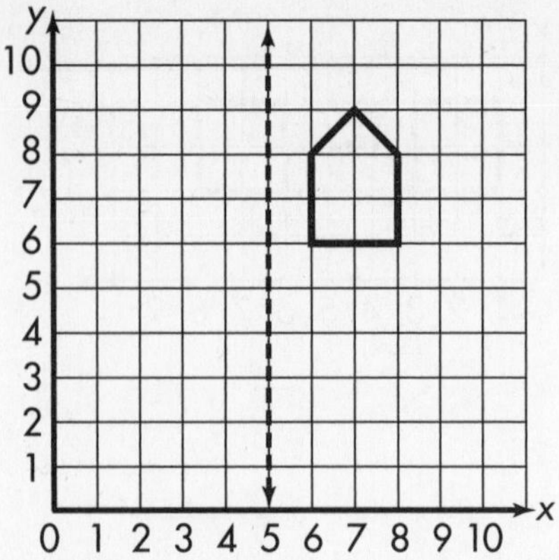

2.

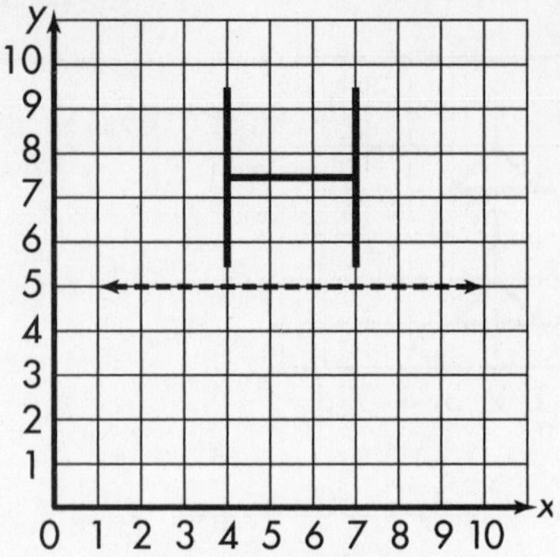

Tell whether the figures in each pair are related by a translation, a reflection, or both.

3.

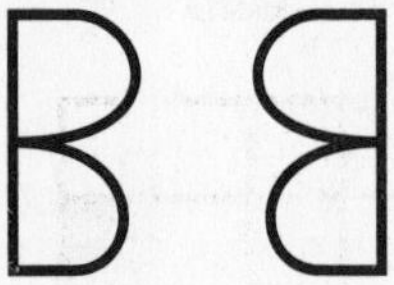

____

4.

____

5. **Think About the Process** Which of the following gives enough information to determine whether the figures A and B have been translated or reflected?

A Figure A is larger than Figure B.

B Figure A and Figure B have the same shape and size.

C Figure A has an identical shape to Figure B.

D Figure A and Figure B are next to each other.

Name ______________________

Practice
19-3

Rotations

Describe whether the figures in each pair are related by a rotation, a translation, or a reflection.

1. 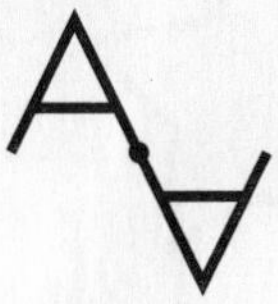

____

2. 

____

3. If the figure at the right is rotated 90° around the point shown, which of the figures below could be the result?

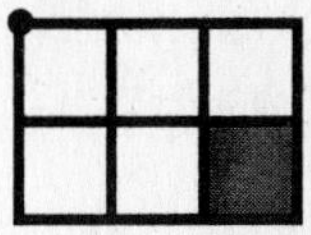

A 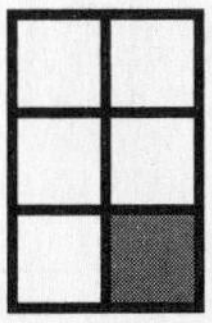

B 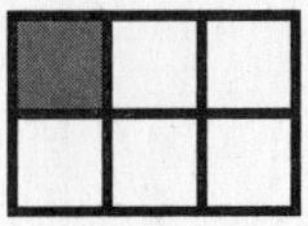

C 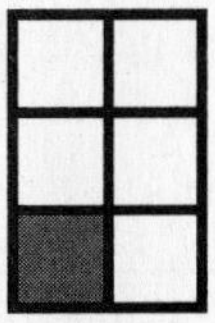

D 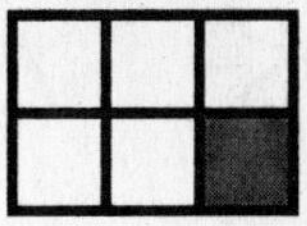

4. **Explain It** Mark says that the figure at the right is a reflection. Faith says that it is a rotation. Who is correct? Explain.

____

____

____

____

____

Name ___________________________

Practice 19-4

Congruence

Tell whether the following figures are congruent or not.

1. 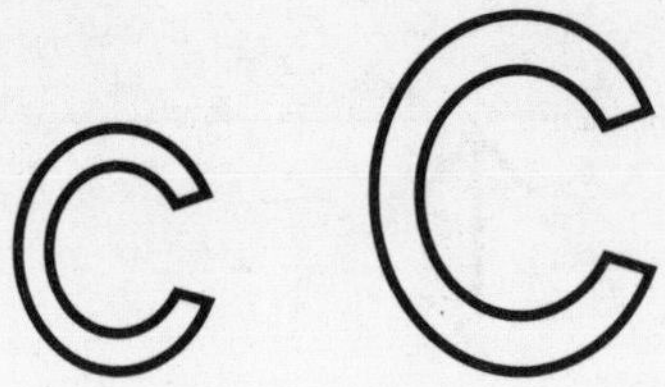

____

2. 

____

Identify each transformation. If not a transformation, explain why.

3. 

____

____

4. 

____

____

5. **Reasonableness** Which of the following situations uses an example of congruent figures?

   A A baker uses two sizes of loaf pans.

   B The fifth-grade math book is wider than the fourth-grade book.

   C You give five friends each a quarter.

   D Two pencils are sharpened, the other two are not.

6. **Explain It** If two triangles are congruent, do they both have the same side lengths? Explain.

____

____

____

Name ______________________

Practice
19-5

Symmetry

For **1** through **4**, tell if the figure has line symmetry, rotational symmetry, or both. If it has line symmetry, how many lines of symmetry are there? If it has rotational symmetry, what is the smallest rotation that will rotate the figure onto itself?

1. 

____

2. 

____

3. 

____

____

4. 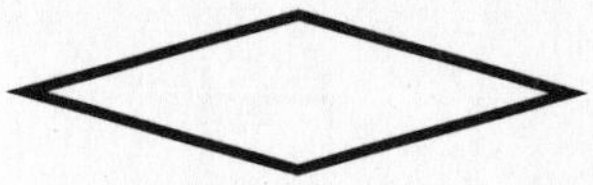

____

____

For **5** and **6**, copy the figure. Then complete the figure so the dashed line is a line of symmetry.

5. 

6. 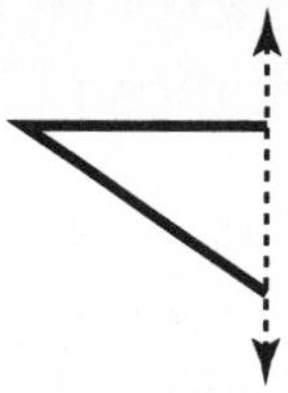

7. Does any rectangle rotate onto itself in less than a half-turn?

____

____

8. Draw a Picture Draw a quadrilateral that has neither line symmetry nor rotational symmetry.

Name ____________________

Problem Solving: Use Objects

1. Is the following a pentomino? Explain.

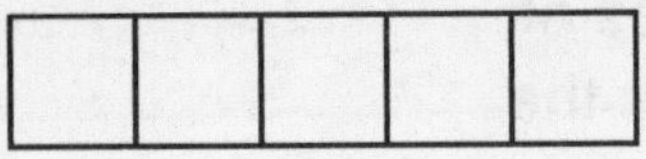

____

____

Tell whether the pentominoes in each pair are related by a reflection or a rotation.

2.

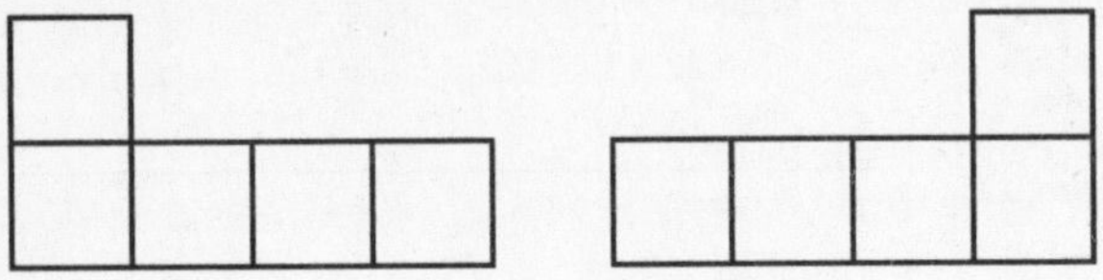

____

3.

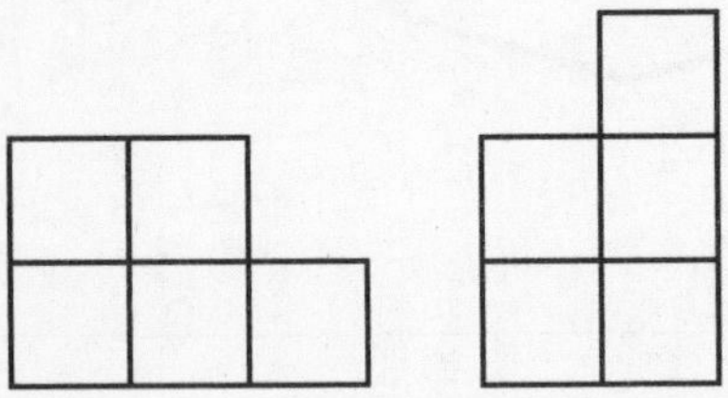

____

4. How many possible different pentominoes can be formed?

A 3 **B** 7 **C** 10 **D** 12

5. **Explain It** Use objects to build pentominoes with 1 square in each row. How many of these kinds of pentominoes can be built? Explain.

____

____

____

Name ______________________

Practice
20-1

Outcomes

The coach is trying to decide in what order Jane, Pete, and Lou will run a relay race.

1. Complete the tree diagram below to show the sample space.

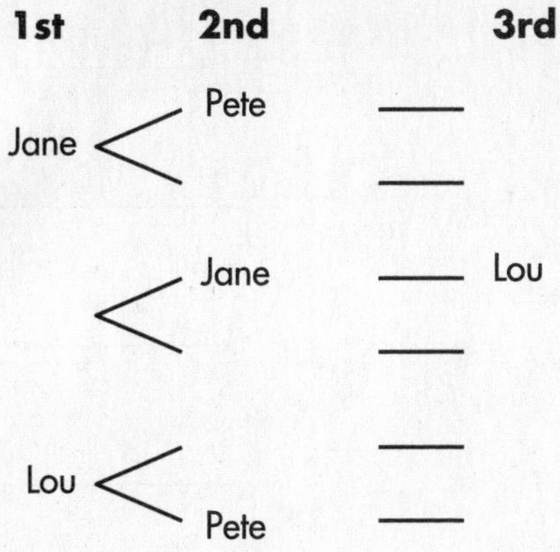

2. How many possible outcomes are there in the sample space? ________

3. After the first runner is chosen, how many choices are there for the second runner? ________

4. **Reasonableness** Tom, Bill, John, and Ed are running for school president. The person in second place automatically becomes vice-president. How many possible outcomes are there in the sample space?

A 6 **B** 9 **C** 10 **D** 12

5. **Explain It** The weather tomorrow could be sunny, cloudy, rainy, or snowy. Is there a 1 out of 4 chance of the weather being sunny?

____

____

Name ______________________________

Practice
20-2

Writing Probability as a Fraction

Tom put 4 yellow marbles, 2 blue marbles, 6 red marbles, and 5 black marbles in a bag.

1. Find *P*(yellow). ____________

2. Find *P*(blue). ____________

3. Find *P*(black). ____________

4. Find *P*(red). ____________

A bag contains 12 slips of paper of the same size. Each slip has one number on it, 1–12.

5. Find *P*(even number). ____________

6. Find *P*(a number less than 6). ____________

7. Find *P*(an odd number). ____________

8. Find *P*(a number greater than 8). ____________

9. Describe an impossible event.

____

10. A cube has 6 sides and is numbered 1 through 6. If the cube is tossed, what is the probability that a 3 will be tossed?

A $\frac{1}{6}$ **B** $\frac{2}{6}$ **C** $\frac{3}{6}$ **D** $\frac{6}{6}$

11. Explain It Explain the probability of tossing a prime number when you toss the cube with numbers 1 through 6.

____

____

Name ______________________

Practice 20-3

Experiments and Predictions

Write each of the following as a fraction in lowest terms.

1. 20 out of 60 ________

2. 16 out of 64 ________

3. 24 out of 60 ________

The table below shows data from the woodshop classes at Jones Elementary School. Students had the choice of making a shelf, a chair, or a birdhouse.

Project	Number of students
Shelf	15
Chair	25
Birdhouse	20

4. What is the total number of students who were taking a woodshop class? ________

5. What is the probability that someone will make a chair? a birdhouse? ________

6. Predict how many students will make a shelf if there are 180 students in the woodshop class. ________

7. **Reasonableness** Using the letters in the word ELEMENTARY, find the probability of choosing a letter that is not E.

A $\frac{3}{10}$

B $\frac{5}{10}$

C $\frac{7}{10}$

D $\frac{9}{10}$

8. **Explain It** If $\frac{2}{3}$ of the 45 customers in the past hour bought a cup of coffee, predict the number of cups that will be sold in the next 3 hours if sales continue at the same level.

____

Name ______________________

Practice

20-4

Problem Solving: Solve a Simpler Problem

Solve the simpler problems. Use the solutions to help you solve the original problem.

1. Reggie is designing a triangular magazine rack with 5 shelves. The top shelf will hold 1 magazine. The second shelf will hold 3 magazines, and the third shelf will hold 5 magazines. This pattern continues to the bottom shelf. How many magazines will the magazine rack hold altogether?

Simpler Problem What is the pattern?

____

____

How many magazines will the fourth shelf hold? __________

How many magazines will the bottom shelf hold? __________

Solution:

____

____

2. At the deli, you receive 1 free sub after you buy 8 subs. How many free subs will you receive from the deli if you buy 24 subs?

____

3. The chef has 5 different kinds of pasta and 3 different flavors of sauce. How many different meals is she able to make?

____

____